Look What You've
Done To Me,
Carter Swinton

Look What You've Done To Me, Carter Swinton

Lily Dancèr

TATE PUBLISHING
AND ENTERPRISES, LLC

Published by Tate Publishing & Enterprises, LLC
127 E. Trade Center Terrace | Mustang, Oklahoma 73064 USA
1.888.361.9473 | www.tatepublishing.com

Tate Publishing is committed to excellence in the publishing industry. The company reflects the philosophy established by the founders, based on Psalm 68:11,
"The Lord gave the word and great was the company of those who published it."

Book design copyright © 2014 by Tate Publishing, LLC. All rights reserved.
Cover design by Errol Villamante
Interior design by Mary Jean Archival

Published in the United States of America

ISBN: 978-1-62510-846-3
Biography & Autobiography / Personal Memoirs
14.10.13

Acknowledgments

Of course, *all* my friends who at some point had to hear about the Carter Swinton drama countless times. My mom and my dad for always listening to me and offering advice even though I didn't like it. Most of all, to my sister for her never-ending patience to listen. And she heard an earful, more than anyone else, because I lived with her. In response to me telling her that my book needs major editing from someone who doesn't know the Carter story, my sister said, "Who on earth do you know who doesn't know the Carter story?"

Prologue

Let me tell you a story. There was a little girl with so much love in her heart. She had so much love to give, but when she gave her love, people thought she was out of the ordinary, too good to be true. "Who has the time or energy to truly care about other's well-being and happiness all the time?" people would ask. "She's too good, too good for me," she'd hear.

As she got older, the love in her heart became even stronger. She knew that loving people whole-heartedly wasn't just a phase. This was her destiny. To make people feel good, even if they weren't willing or capable of returning the love. She was never deterred when people were hesitant to accept her sincerity or when people attributed her goodness to innocence and being naïve. "If only she knew how the world worked," people would say. But, she never gave up on anyone.

One day, she unexpectedly met the man of her dreams. The only problem was that he wasn't sure if she was the girl of his dreams. He decided to get to know her and soon discovered her passion to give love unconditionally. He was intrigued yet intimidated by this girl. He chose to admire her from a distance, never making a commitment to close the gap but also never quite severing the ties. She was a blessing in his life, no one like her, but he didn't know what to do with her.

He would witness her surrounded by negativity and still choose not to succumb to it. He witnessed her walk to the beat of her own drum, no matter what. It was new to him, something he didn't know how to incorporate into his life. "She won't fit in, but I really like her," he would think. As this boy's heart and mind fought over what he should do, his fluctuating feelings unintentionally sent mixed messages to the girl and confused her. She already knew she loved him, no doubts in her mind, so she didn't understand why or how he didn't know exactly what he wanted, why he couldn't give her a straight answer.

Over the years, her love for him grew stronger while his constantly wavered. He pushed her away when he was distracted with life and pulled her back in when he realized how much he missed her. Through all this, she never stopped loving him. Sometimes, she wondered if he knew the depth of her love.

Chapter 1

What was I supposed to think when I'd never felt this way before? Was I truly supposed to be able to decipher these feelings at the age of seventeen? Saturday, July 15, 2000 at 12:15 p.m. was the start of a roller-coaster ride that lasted ten years. My life would *never* be the same after that day.

I was fresh out of high school. Awkward, shy, and a naïve schoolgirl. I had never once dated. In addition, I was the daughter of Egyptian immigrants, which meant I had to learn about boys on my own. In my parents' foreign eyes, girls just waited until boys pursued them—the end. I was clueless about boys.

Over the years, I had many crushes, to no avail. They clearly meant nothing because when I saw *him*, the world stopped, and all I saw was *him* looking at me staring at *him*. He was gorgeous—exactly what I dreamed my husband would look like. Actually, he looked even better than what I imagined. Killer eyes like the blue of a pristine ocean and that look. That's all I saw. That's all I needed to see to make me melt, to make me feel my world was complete, to make me feel like a winner.

In that instant, I knew I had fallen in love. I just wanted to get lost in us. I knew I wanted this guy in my life, forever. I just had to have him. From that day forward, I experienced every emotion known to man, and even some that probably don't exist.

Imagine an elephant rushing toward you, obstructing your view of anything with its sheer size. Picture it trumpeting in your face and shattering your eardrums, all the while blowing strong gusts of air that leave you gasping. All your senses are stimulated, and your adrenaline is pumping, but you're frozen in place. You are mesmerized by the beauty and power of the creature to the point that you can't look away. It's fascinating and amazing, but also intimidating and overwhelming.

You're witnessing God's beautiful creation in awe. It's a powerful whirlwind of positive emotions. What can you do in that situation? It's too much, too fast.

That's exactly what overcame me the instant we locked eyes. That intense feeling did not subside in the least over the next ten years despite our distance and lack of interaction. With each passing year, additional elephants joined the stampede, and my passion grew stronger; I was even more intrigued and in awe. In the last few months of our relationship, all I could hear and see were elephants.

I had hope when there should have been none. I had faith when no one else did. I was optimistic while everyone else was pessimistic. I saw the glass half full rather than half empty. I was positive, but everyone else was negative. I defied all odds because I believed deep down that my gut feeling could not fail me. I was going to ride out this wave no matter where it took me, just as long as I got what I wanted in the end. I wanted to be in control. But that's not how life works. My plan is not God's plan.

Those killer eyes—so what? Now I know better. Gorgeous for what? What good is it to be good-looking? So that when we argue I see a pretty face and succumb to it? Looks aren't everything, I learned ten years too late. I have a theory. Sometimes I think that

I just want to be with an extremely good-looking jerk to make up for all those years during my childhood when I got made fun of by good-looking jerks. But life isn't about payback—it's about paying forward.I wish I had a good reason for falling in love—or maybe it was lust—with this guy, but I don't. Sometimes circumstances surrounding love can't be explained. In my ten-year roller-coaster ride, this was an inexplicable phenomenon. With all the pain and red flags, I still couldn't stop the ride and let go. All I know is that I was jamming my foot into a door that should have been shut long ago.

Of course, this is an observation that can only come about in hindsight. Hindsight is always 20/20. God communicates with us daily, even momentarily. Apparently, I chose to ignore His messages because I was adamant about keeping that remarkable herd of elephants. Their majestic beauty overpowered my scruples. Unfortunately, my stubborn nature led me to fall away from God, and ultimately make some of the worst decisions of my life.

Nevertheless, I am an optimist, and I can say that I came away from this situation as a wonderful storyteller and entertainer because of my plethora of stories. My life was truly tantamount to a reality TV show. Look what you've done to me, Carter Swinton.

Chapter 2

I was on a bus full of obnoxious children, wondering why we hadn't left yet. We were half an hour behind schedule. I was seventeen, very shy, and right out of high school. My mom made the decision for me to be a camp counselor for our church camp so I could meet new people. I reluctantly agreed. I didn't need to meet anyone new. I had all my high school friends. Besides, church people are cliquey.

Finally, I heard that we were waiting for the other counselor, Carter Swinton, to arrive. Then the news changed. He woke up late and decided to drive himself to camp instead of taking the school bus with the campers. Ugh! I already didn't like the sound of this camp. The counselors weren't even responsible enough to arrive on time. *Remind me to give this guy a dirty look when I meet him since I'm too shy to have a talk with him.*

When we arrived at the camp, I was groggy and disheveled from the long ride. I stepped off the bus, holding my pillow, and saw him. His wide stance showing his ease of the world and his folded arms showing off his muscular arms. Not to mention his white t-shirt with blue lettering that brought out the gleam in his blue eyes.

He saw me too. What he saw, I'm not sure because I was wearing a pastel rainbow striped shirt and high waisted flare jeans with pockets only on the ankles, a complete fashion faux pas. We held each other's gaze for what seemed like an eternity. No one else existed in that brief moment.

The girl he was talking to faded into the distance. I had never been overcome with emotion as much as I was that moment. I knew I wanted this boy in my life forever, whether as a friend or, preferably, my husband. It was love at first sight, and every other sight afterward.

We had an immediate connection. We had a connection that sparked just at the thought of it. That must be Carter Swinton. There was no way for me to be mad at him. He was hot, and he clearly thought I was hot. Well, at least I made a friend, even though I knew every girl at camp would hate me. New girl and the camp hottie are not a good combination if you want to make girlfriends.

Here at camp was where the black magic started. My life would be changed forever, and not in a good way. I had no way of knowing that Carter Swinton would be the bane of my existence. I had no idea that someone who brought me such joy could also bring me such pain. I had no idea that I could hate and love someone all at once. I had no idea that my life would be at the mercy of a single boy, holding the joystick that controlled my life. I had no idea that obsession was a reality and that I would become a victim to its harsh grasp. I had no idea how to get over him. Look what you've done to me, Carter Swinton.

Day 1 of camp:

I was an observer. I didn't know anyone at all. Carter came over to talk to me for a bit and I relaxed. At least I had one person to talk to. Out of the corner of my eye, I noticed a girl giving me a dirty look. It was the same girl he was talking to before Carter and I locked eyes. I made a note to myself to avoid her for the rest of the week. She was sure to be trouble.

As I walked around camp that day, I noticed quite a few of the older female campers eyeing Carter and said a quick thank you to God for arranging that I work with the youngest girls, ages five and six, surely drama-free. Yes, he was *that* good looking.

His piercing, crystal blue eyes made girls stumble in their footsteps, the pain of longing exposed. He exuded an air of confidence that resonated with just about every female, adult or teen, at camp, including myself. Unfortunately, at the age of 17, I mistook his swagger for a desirable attribute rather than note it as a shortcoming and sign of insecurity, which led to many of our arguments in the future.

That night, in preparation for the next day's activities, the staff had to carry boxes up the hill to the field. As I walked by Carter, he said, "It sure would be nice to have you link arms with me." I giggled and walked right past. Instead, that girl rushed over and grabbed his arm stealing his attention.

Settling into my cabin for the night, I was excited to get to know my adorable campers. As we were going around talking about our favorite activities that day, Nanette, a darling camper said, "He's my cousin." Not understanding who she was talking about, I asked, "Who's your cousin?" "Carter Swinton, the boy who likes you," she said proudly. Could you blame me for being skeptical? Why would she entrust me with this jewel of information? I had only met Nanette today, Carter and I had very few interactions so far, and she was six. How could she possibly know?

On the one hand, I was giving her comment way too much weight. On the other hand, I thought she was just being a kid and joking. Nah. I was going to believe her. From psychology class, I remembered that kids have a gift to sift through the noise of life and have the capability to succinctly see people's true intentions because their innocence hasn't been skewed yet. How strange

14

that with five cabins for girls, his cousin Nanette was in mine. Surely, it was a sign. With that, I went to bed beaming.

Day 2 of camp:

Although the day was cloudy, my happiness radiated heat. How I wish I could go back to the days when an off-hand comment made by a six year old was the highlight of my day.

Today was the day when we'd be paired off with another group for daily activities for the rest of the week. I held my breath, silently reciting lyrics: "wishing and hoping and thinking and praying, planning and dreaming," that I'd be paired up with Carter.

An involuntary excited wiggle revealed my uncontainable delight when my wish came true. Simultaneously, as if on cue, "dirty look" girl sent me a snide look. I was too young and inexperienced to fathom what that look encompassed. But, I knew enough to know that my every move would be scrutinized. I made a mental note to silently sing that song as a good luck charm. Carter and I would be alone for several hours a day, if you didn't include our campers. I was like a little kid in a candy store, simply and obviously excited all the time.

Already Carter and I shared intimate smiles during activity time. Our campers weren't as clueless as I thought. They kept teasing us. "You guys love each other," the kids chanted. Carter was so cool, calm and collected while I was giddy and transparent. Out of the blue, he grabbed me, dipped me, and kissed me, in front of the kids. The kids gasped. What they didn't see was that Carter placed his thumb on my lips, and kissed his thumb. The way his hands were placed on my face gave the illusion that he was tenderly holding me close to him.

That was my first kiss. To this day, as silly as it may be, I still consider that my first passionate kiss. The magical feeling that lingered after his touch was more powerful than anyone else's.

Later that night, we sang songs by the campfire. Carter and I sat next to each other. It was a chilly night, but I wasn't sure if I was shivering out of sheer nervousness of being so close to him or because I was literally cold. He offered me his jacket and of course, I declined it. I wasn't trying to be prideful. I just shut down in the presence of Carter. Eventually, he wrapped his jacket around me. The combination of the heat from the fire, the warmth of the jacket and "dirty look" girl's scorching death stare, stopped my shivering.

I went to bed in his jacket, taking in every smell. I have no idea what cologne it was but even now, any hint of that scent and I'm brought back to my camp days with Carter.

Day 3 at camp:

What more could a girl want? In two days, I had already won the heartthrob, been "kissed," been seen wearing his jacket, and had exclusive time with the man I loved.

I came to breakfast in his jacket amidst a chorus of gasps from the older female campers and counselors, the loudest gasp from "dirty look" girl. I was cold so I wore his jacket. I wasn't trying to show off or prove anything. Immediately, the image of sweet Sandy coming to school in hot shot Danny's jacket, confirming they were going steady to a shocked student body, in the movie *Grease*, came to mind.

During activity time, one of my five-year old campers would not leave my side. She was getting homesick and clung to my hand for dear life. As Carter made his way over to me for our usual chats, the little girl grabbed his hand as well. Her face immediately lit up. "I wanna jump in the air!" she exclaimed with glee. Holding each of her hands, continuing our conversation, we walked around lifting her in the air. *What great parents we'd make.* I just knew that it would only be a matter of time before his masculine fingers would be wrapped around my delicate hand.

We're destined to be together, was all I could think at the time. Looking back, I was too naïve to notice the theme of barriers between us. First, his thumb getting in the way of a passionate kiss and now a child getting in between our hands. If only I had known that this was a foreshadowing of the next ten years, maybe I would have been more sensible.

That night, I couldn't sleep. Thoughts of Carter were keeping me up so I went for a walk and found myself at the swings. I sat there pondering the last three days. *Had it really only been three days since I fell in love? Was I acting irrational over a boy?* I already felt a wave of nausea at the thought of leaving Carter at the end of the week.

My thoughts were interrupted by someone pushing my swing. I looked back, elated to see Carter. "Do you need a push?" he considerately asked. "I'm a big girl. I can do it myself," I curtly responded. *Lily! Why are you sabotaging every opportunity with Carter?* He tried again. "Why are you out here so late?" "I can't sleep," I said. He went back to his cabin and brought me his CD player with a CD of the sounds of the ocean. "This always helps me sleep," he said with a soft smile on his face.

Carter pushing me on the swing resonated deeply with me. Years later, while out to dinner with my family, waiting for our food, I started doodling on the paper tablecloth only to have it become a masterpiece: a picture of Carter pushing me on the swing. It was as if my hands had a mind of their own. By no means am I an artist, but I became one that evening.

I jotted down the name of the CD before returning it to him the next day in order to buy it the minute I got home. I still have trouble sleeping. Carter still runs through my mind each night. I can't imagine how many pairs of running shoes he's gone through over the years in my thoughts. I've tried everything from spraying lavender on my sheets to sleeping pills and the only thing that gets me remotely close to sleep is that treasured CD of ocean sounds.

A rustle of the leaves surprised us and we turned to see "dirty look" girl. "Carter, let's go talk," she adamantly demanded. "Hope you get some rest," Carter said, unwillingly leaving. "Thanks," I said crestfallen. The wheels started turning in my head. *He clearly likes me but goes off with "dirty look" girl whenever she insists. Do I need to be rude and nasty to get the boy of my dreams? If so, how could I transform myself when I'm just a demure little girl?*

Day 4 at camp:

I woke up before my alarm clock. I wanted to look particularly nice for Carter so I decided to take a quick shower before my campers woke up. I took my clothes off, wrapped myself in a towel, stepped out of the cabin, and walked the short distance to the community female bathrooms, knowing no one would be up to see me in my lack of clothes. As I quickly washed my hair, while humming Dusty Springfield's, *Wishing and Hoping*, I thought about what I'd wear that day.

Wrapping the towel around myself, I casually walked out of the bathroom not stopping to make sure I was still the only one up. I impulsively turned as I passed Carter's cabin, which happened to be across from the bathrooms, not expecting to see him.

But, there he was just staring at me with an allusive grin. I simultaneously hiked up the bottom of my towel to my upper thigh and lowered the top portion to just above my areolas, showing off what little cleavage I had. Where this audacity came from, I had no idea.

In that moment, I wanted his eyes on me forever and I was willing to be naughty. Oh, my parents would be upset if they knew the shy little girl they raised to have good morals was acting this way. Our brief tryst ended as I came to my wits, and looked away, even though I could feel his yearning eyes burning a hole through my towel, seductively undressing me as I walked away.

Embarrassed about my bold behavior earlier, I kept my distance from Carter and stole furtive looks at him during activity time, making lanyards. Carter was using a clear lanyard speckled with silver and gold glitter. He dropped one of his strings and never picked it up. I stowed that information in my mind until an hour later when we moved on to lunch. As we seated ourselves in the mess hall, I excused myself to use the bathroom only to go pick up the lanyard string he dropped unnoticed. I quickly pocketed the string, pleased with myself for being sneaky.

To this day, I have that lanyard string. It's glued inside a notebook above a dated caption describing where I found it. Back then, I thought my actions were harmless. Since that week in July, I've been to numerous counselors only to be told the same thing, "I can't help you as long as you hold on to that string. Throw it away, then we can make progress."

Stubbornly, I continue holding on to it. I *can't* bear to throw it away. I once threw the notebook away and had unsettling sleep dreaming about it. The instant I woke up, I dug it out of the trash, put it in its rightful place, my closet, where it still resides ten years later.

Day 5 at camp:

The day had come for swimming Olympics. Anything to reveal my trim figure, I excitedly wore my green checkered boy short bikini, hideous now looking back at it. Carter wouldn't let me forget my lack of fashion sense either, years down the road. Carter offered to rub sunscreen on my back; I shyly declined. A few minutes later, he offered to rub sunscreen on my front. I nervously glanced away. He was so forward. I wasn't playing hard to get; I just didn't know what to do. This was my first experience of a guy liking me at all. I'd never had male attention before this, let alone the attention of the hottest guy around.

Out of the corner of my eye, I could see "dirty look" girl smirk. Looked like she had plans to win Carter over. Carter walked over to her and they chatted. I started taking notice of how he would ditch me for that girl every time he didn't get what he wanted with me.

Instead of attributing his overcompensating actions to a lack of insecurity, I made myself the scapegoat. It was my fault he didn't spend more time with me. It was my actions that pushed him away. This sense of inadequacy followed me for the next ten years and directed my actions with him. I never learned. Instead, I fell further into the hole I was digging and he was never there to help me out like I imagined he would.

Later that afternoon, I worked with another counselor, Eric, who I later found out, was Carter's cousin. I hadn't even noticed him all week. I was too distracted by his sweet-talking cousin. Eric and I hit it off, leaving no traces of the shy, demure girl who surfaced around Carter. Eric confessed that he had been watching me since he first laid eyes on me, but never made any moves because Carter seemed interested.

He was purposely keeping his distance from me to avoid arguing with his cousin over a girl. He was so upset that he wasn't around to meet me first. Apparently, I was his ideal woman. Now my best friend, ten years later, he never fails to remind me that we should be together; if only he met me before Carter to sweep me off my feet.

Lying in bed that night, thoughts were swirling. *I was completely myself around Eric. He's attractive but not as attractive as Carter. Am I obsessed with Carter or is it love? I only have two more days at camp.* I tried to count sheep to no avail. I tried to count my thoughts, but that ended up a futile effort as well. When I finally fell into a deep sleep, my dreams were filled with Carter.

Day 6 at camp:

I had another opportunity to show off my trim figure during field trip day to the waterpark. I wasn't vain, but I knew, that I was in the best shape at camp, by far.

I sat next to Nanette on the bus, while Carter sat next to "dirty look" girl. I couldn't hear what they were talking about, but my ears perked up when I heard my name. Carter was bringing me up in conversation and I could see that the girl was annoyed. He kept glancing my way, but all I could do was shrug my shoulders, lower my eyes, and bashfully smile. I wasn't making it easy for him. I always found a way to run and hide.

Nanette had been squirming, excitedly chatting with her new friends about what they would do at the waterpark. Suddenly, she turned to me and joyously asked, "Can you marry Carter? I want you to be in my family." Already the family approves. Who cares that she's a six year old? It's still approval. Thankfully, no one noticed my first ever sinister grin. Something was changing inside of me. I wasn't going to be timid little Lily anymore.

At the waterpark, as usual, I went off solo. I didn't want to be around Eric in fear that Carter would think I liked him, and I obviously couldn't spend time with any girls. They all avoided me like the plague ever since they noticed Carter's attraction to me. I resigned myself to the lazy river that wrapped around the perimeter of the waterpark. From my inner tube, I was able to spy on Carter.

"Dirty look" girl snagged Carter the moment we got off the bus and wouldn't leave his side. He didn't seem unhappy, but he didn't seem too thrilled either. Every time Carter spotted me in the lazy river, no matter what he was doing, he stopped to enthusiastically wave to me. I never picked up the hint to get out and join him.

I don't know if my lack of assertiveness was due to my traditional upbringing or my perceived notion that men are supposed to incessantly chase the girl, like in romantic movies. Either way, neither of those principles were getting me anywhere.

The day was coming to a close. My skin was shriveled beyond belief. I spent the entire time in the lazy river with my dysfunctional thoughts. *Why won't Carter join me in the river? How can I convince him that he wants to marry me? What will I do after tomorrow? I can't live without him!*

That night I vowed to be more proactive and be an active participant in my future. I was going to be upfront with Carter. I was going to make a move. "Dirty look" girl was not going to take Carter from me.

Day 7 at camp:

Breakfast then the bus ride home. I was nervous about what I was going to do. I wanted breakfast to last forever so I could stare at Carter comfortably from a safe distance. I also wanted breakfast to end to prove to myself that I could go after what I want.

After every dish was washed and all the tables wiped down, I painstakingly and awkwardly walked over to Carter. "Can I get a ride home with you? I'm on your way home," I uneasily said. As if I hadn't stayed up all night envisioning this moment, with a smile Carter immediately said, "Sure." I exhaled, a little too loudly, cognizant that I was seconds away from passing out if I held my breath any longer. Pleased with myself, I went back to the cabin and packed my bag, ready for an adrenaline crammed drive home.

The campers were loading the bus, saving seats, and animat-edly chattering with their newfound friends. Before Nanette dis-appeared from my sight, she squeezed me tightly. "I'll miss you, Lily. Please, please, please be part of our family," she pleaded. "I'll do my best," I replied. With a huge grin, she ran off and joined her friends.

Impatiently awaiting the ride home with Carter, the last camper finally entered the bus, the doors closed, and the engine started. In just a few moments I would be *completely alone* with Carter, but my thoughts were disturbed as the camp director flagged the bus driver.

Agitated, the director walked over to me and sternly asked, "Why aren't you on the bus? You were the only counselor on the bus. You can't just leave the kids unsupervised. You came on the bus, you leave on the bus." My heart took a nose dive. "I'm sorry," I sullenly said as I took the walk of shame toward the bus, with my tail tucked between my legs. *I just want to spend some time with Carter*, I silently screamed. Once again, the inevitable theme of separation, this time a bus, enlarged the chasm between us.

"Wait!" Carter beckoned. "Can I have your AIM (America Online Instant Messenger) screen name and phone number?" We exchanged information in front of all the other counselors, drawing even more unwanted attention to our magnetism. Not only was "dirty look" girl furious, but now I had the added burden of seeing Eric sulk as his chances of dating me were dwindling right before his eyes. In that instant, my love for drama was cultivated.

His screen name became my password for *all* my logins. I couldn't forget his screen name even if I wanted to. It was a part of my daily life. My passwords ten years later are still linked to Carter. Through the years, we had many flirtatious conversations via instant messenger.

Now, any time I type a password, I welcome flooding memories of Carter, and I can't help but smile. Is that obsession? Is holding on to a nice memory considered not moving on? My therapists insisted that it was unhealthy to place such high value on a few memories. I, on the other hand, chose not to believe them, and continued to evoke memories of Carter any way I possibly could.

I was miserable on the bus. I hugged my pillow, imagining it was Carter. My misery exponentially grew as it crossed my mind that the next opportunity to see Carter would be next summer at camp. I couldn't wait that long.

My first time away from home for an extended period of time, of course my parents were enthusiastically curious about my week. As I explained how much fun camp was to my parents, I started crying. At the mere mention of Carter Swinton, my tear ducts turned on and wouldn't shut off. I had never felt so strongly about anyone before. I missed him so much. There was no way I could wait a whole year.

Chapter 3

I met the man I wanted to marry July 15, 2000. The seven days at camp were the best days of my life. But with no concrete plans to ever see Carter again, I impatiently crossed off dates on my wall calendar each night, counting down the days until next summer when I was sure to see the man I wanted to father my children.

The moment I got home from camp I typed his screen name into AIM, excited to have a link to Carter. But, he was *never* online. *Never.* I became obsessed with waiting for him to show up. I felt like a girl stood up on a date, sitting at a dinner table, eagerly waiting for the man of my dreams to show up. He *never* showed up.

My first year of college would be starting soon, and I couldn't lose any more sleep anticipating his grand appearance. I came up with a plan. I added a mooing cow sound to indicate his entrance online. Finally, having found a solution to my Carter dilemma, I maxed the speaker volume and peeled myself away from the computer screen, confident that my presence was no longer mandatory to catch him online. The mooing cow would beckon me when it was time.

Fast forward two months; September 15, 2000. I hadn't heard from Carter. My life seemed purposeless without him. I found my first white hair and decided it grew in because of the stress of not talking to him, so I named it Carter. I didn't think I'd be able to make it much longer without contact from him. I didn't know what I'd do if I didn't speak to him, but I knew it wouldn't be pretty. It had been too long since I'd seen Carter.

Counting on my mooing cow, I was happy to spend less time glued to the computer. All day and still no alert had sounded. Later that evening, I happened to glance at the screen and saw it. A blinking blue text window. I hadn't heard it. I smoothed my hair back, tidying myself as if it mattered, and sat down in a daze. All summer I had been waiting for this moment. Now that it had arrived, I wished I had more time to prepare what I'd say. About to type, "hello," I saw the time he sent me the message, 2:16 p.m. It was now 8:29 p.m. I quickly checked my speaker volume. It was raised as high as it could go. Something had gone terribly wrong.

In my deep-rooted exhilaration, I misspelled his screen name when I initially typed it in months earlier. All this time, I was expecting a nonexistent person to show up online. "Wat's up," his message read. My mind went blank. *How do I respond to that?* I froze.

As if I didn't have all the time in the world to perfect my message in the blinking blue box, I absurdly wrote, "Hey babe." *What's wrong with me?* His lack of response made me nervous. Forget that I responded more than six hours later. I wanted instant gratification. Two minutes went by. *Oh my gosh! I've ruined things! He doesn't want to talk to me!* Suddenly, the blue blinking box with Carter's response, "Wat u up to?" snapped me out of my foolishness.

No matter how hard I tried, hiding behind the façade of the computer still didn't curb my ridiculous conversation. I was still a giddy girl who couldn't filter her thoughts. Question after silly question poured out of my fingers. Anything to continue the conversation. "What are you doing? Are you leaving for school on Wednesday night? Are you still driving that car? Where are you going?" Somehow he managed to enjoy two hours of chatting with me with a desire to chat again soon. I was elated.

I found a spiral notebook rummaging through my desk drawers, printed the conversation out, dated it, and glued it on the second page. This was the first of many documented conversations. The first page was saved for the captioned lanyard from camp.

Rather than crossing off September 15, 2000 on my calendar, I circled it in bold green marker. I fell back onto my bed, arms spread, stupidly grinning, thinking about what a lucky girl I was. I was already planning the wedding. Clearly, the fine line between dreams and reality were muddled for me.

Chapter 4

After correcting the spelling of his screen name, the mooing cow alert worked just fine. He was *always* online. We started chatting daily, increasing it to multiple times a day within a week. I learned how to get a grip on my anxiety and used the concealment of the computer to my advantage. Shy little Lily wasn't shy through AIM. I learned how to use instant messenger to my advantage, using wait time to manifest perfect lines.

I became a professional flirt, but I have to give recognition where it's due. Without Carter Swinton, I would have no game. We lived far from each other, and our only consistent contact was through instant messenger. I got good at saying the right things to keep him coming back. I was so thrilled that this hot, popular guy was giving me attention.

I went overboard. I printed out all our instant message conversations for the next three years, dated them, and glued them into the notebook. Flipping through the notebook, you'd see an array of colors highlighting all the charming comments he wrote to me.

Ten years later, I still have the notebook, along with other things I collected over the years that have to do with Carter

Swinton. I wouldn't typically consider myself a collector or a pack rat, but in this case, you can call me a Carter Swinton pack rat collector. Anything he touched, said, or had ever been associated with that I could get my hands on, you can bet that I have it in my leopard storage stool saved for Carter memorabilia.

Let me explain what I have in this stool other than the dated and highlighted notebook of online conversations. It started off with the piece of lanyard he was playing with at camp. He touched it and dropped it, and it became a gem to me, probably my most prized possession in my museum of Carter.

I have the piece of paper he wrote his phone number and screen name on that last day of camp. I even have some of his essays from college and his law school entrance essay. Whatever he showed me, I kept. I have the few pictures I took with him and some of my favorite pictures of him that I printed off of Facebook, years after AIM.

Then, there are also pictures that I drew of him, including the masterpiece drawn at the restaurant of Carter pushing me on the swings. I also have a picture I created using rubber stamps while working as a teacher's aide at a preschool. It read, "Carter loves Lily."

Five years after meeting Carter, I began my career as a high school math teacher. During my first year of teaching, I had no filter; my students were my outlet and knew the entire Carter saga. One day, one of my female students gave me a letter from her mother empathizing with my situation, yet vehemently explaining why I should stay away from Carter. I knew I had crossed a line.

My personal life was becoming dinner conversation at home for my students. I still kept that note. It's in the leopard stool. I have countless pros and cons lists. Every single voice mail he left me, I have recorded on a cassette tape. That's in the stool too. It's a constant stream of Carter's voice that I can listen to when I miss him. I was officially love-crazed, maybe even obsessed.

Chapter 5

Carter became my cyber life. Meanwhile, in real life, I was blossoming. I was becoming a swan, apparent by all the sudden attention I was getting from boys.

In October, Ray Nossing, a high school friend, took the leap and asked me out. I figured it couldn't hurt to date. This way I'd be more experienced when Carter, my prince in shining armor, came for me. Ray was my first boyfriend. I never told him about Carter. I finally, distinctly understood Rose's words in *Titanic*, "A woman's heart is a deep ocean of secrets." We made it through our first month, still committed to making it work.

Carter was busy with college, inaccessible to me. Attending University of Southern California, USC, made him quite the snob and social butterfly. He joined a fraternity and every club and intramural sport possible. He was practically unreachable. The boy I fell in love with was becoming the stereotypical college student: sports and girls all day, partying and more girls all night.

I, on the other hand, didn't epitomize the clichéd college girl; I held on to my innocence. Our online chats were dwindling and they weren't as exciting as before. Yet, I still stayed up each night just a little too late hoping I'd at least get a "good night" from Carter. Still, Ray had no idea Carter existed.

When Carter found himself in my dreams more than Ray did, I started worrying. *I really like Ray. I know I like Carter more. I love Carter.* Immaturely, I pushed those thoughts away, hoping my irrationality would disappear on its own since Ray and I were doing well. Until Thanksgiving.

Carter came home from school. I was supposed to spend the entire weekend with Ray; but Carter called and asked to spend the weekend with me, knowing quite well that I had a boyfriend. All my initial feelings of longing resurfaced. Any committed girl would have said, "No way," but I wanted to see Carter so badly I said, "Yes." I easily canceled my plans to go to Disneyland and the beach with Ray and hung out with Carter, without any remorse whatsoever.

Of course, Ray called me, heartbroken, while I was hanging out with Carter. "Lily, I really want to see you. Can I please come over and just spend a little time with you tonight? Even a few hours?" Ray implored, as Carter scandalously smirked at me. The hurt in Ray's voice was heart wrenching. It would have been easier to ignore his phone call. Rudely, I responded with, "No, it's not a good idea for us to spend so much time together. I'm busy." I never told him why I canceled so suddenly on him.

How quickly I forgot about Ray. I had eyes only for Carter. Carter knew I was a good girl; he knew how to work this good girl really well. Line after sugar coated line melodiously floated from his lips. "I'm gonna treat you like your body begs to be treated. I enjoy the finer things in life; I enjoy you." In the midst of his charming comments, his experienced hands found their way to my back, giving me a sensual massage.

Shortly afterwards, we jumped into the hot tub, where he brought out some beers. We were only 18, not of drinking age. Then he kissed me. My very first kiss, other than the one at camp. He was corrupting me in every way.

31

Ray and I had a very innocent relationship. We interpreted intimacy as holding hands and going to events, just spending time together. It had been a month and we still hadn't kissed.

Carter Swinton gave me my very first kiss! We were in the hot tub, but if we were standing up, I'm sure my leg would have magically lifted like in romantic movies. I was nervous I wouldn't be any good. I initially backed away, embarrassed by my inexperience. He mistook that for playfulness and leaned in with more desire, determined to lock lips. The sparks that flew when his lips gently brushed mine were enough for a decent Fourth of July celebration. I looked at him longingly, never wanting the night to end.

After that fabulous weekend with Carter, my most memorable Thanksgiving, I knew I wouldn't see him again for a while, but I didn't care. I was floating too high for anyone to reach me. It reminded me of a poem I read.

> "I climbed up the door and opened the stairs
> I said my pajamas and put on my prayers
> I turned off the bed and crawled into the light
> And all because you kissed me good night"

Carter kissed me before my very own boyfriend. Worst girlfriend ever! I risked losing a wonderful boyfriend to a quick fling. Ray truly loved me; he forgave me when I guiltily told him weeks later. Throughout our two-year relationship, I never stopped talking to Carter, but I never told Ray of my continued contact.

When we finally broke up, for other reasons, but mostly because of Carter, I was relieved. It was as if I was waiting for Ray to leave me. Now I could begin my conquest to get Carter Swinton to become my boyfriend.

Chapter 6

Meanwhile, in the dorms, my roommate and best friend, Anna, was getting fed up with me. I didn't own a computer or a laptop all through college. She was nice enough to let me borrow hers whenever I wanted. I'm sure a few months into the year she wanted to revoke her offer. I used her laptop to chat with Carter at all hours of the night, even more than I did for writing papers. Even worse, I used her ink to print out our conversations.

Everyone who lived in the same suite, at least fourteen other girls, knew the entire story about Carter and would come into our room to help me figure out what was best to say over instant messenger. The girls would gather around me in a circle bickering over whose smart-aleck comment I should use.

More often than not, the comments they offered were completely off the wall, as if living vicariously through my chats gave them courage to say whatever nonsense they wanted. Sometimes we would stay up so late Anna would stand with her hands on her hips, head cocked to the side, and yell at us to go to bed.

Carter: I thought I saw your car today and got happy, but
it wasn't you so I got sad
Me: awww

I typed that and quickly deleted it. I had to confer with my posse of girls. We had to vote on it and discuss the pros and cons of that response.

Mandy: That's so girly. Play hard to get. How about typing, "Why would I be at USC? There's nothing there for me."
Carrie: No way! That's mean. Lily doesn't want to push him away. What about, "Look for my car tomorrow, I'll be around." And you have to put a happy face.
Me: But, I have class tomorrow and I have to study.
Carrie: So what! Just miss class!
Dena: Umm…why don't you just say, "I'm sad it wasn't my car too."
Me: Ohhh, I kinda like that
Mandy: You guys are lame. So cheesy.
Me: Whatever, I'm typing that.
Anna: Are you seriously still talking about Carter's one comment? Go to bed! He's just a flirt and doesn't mean anything. I need to sleep! It's freakin' 2 am and I have a midterm tomorrow at 8 in the morning.
Me: Ok ok ok. Let me just type this and I'll shut the laptop down.

After the lengthy discussion over a simple response, I was satisfied with the comment choice we made and eagerly awaited his answer. A few uneventful minutes passed while Anna bore holes through us with her burning looks of annoyance. Not wanting to deal with the wrath of Anna, my friends reluctantly left me.

I turned my back to Anna trying to avoid eye contact, my elbow on the desk, head propped on my palm, and prayed Carter would respond soon. Finally, as I was dozing off, the ping of his response jolted me awake.

I couldn't wait to see what he had to say. "Sorry, I got busy. I gotta go." *Aghhh. I waited too long to respond.* All that work and lack of sleep for nothing. Throwing a pillow at me from her half-slumber, Anna exasperatedly said, "Woman! Have you no consideration?! Sleep!! Are you satisfied? Will you finally go to bed now? I told you he's just a talker," she coaxed, the only voice of reason within my friends.

Everyone was on my side, helping me flirt with this guy, trying to convince him to be more than just a chat buddy. Freshman year was coming to a close, and still no one had met Carter Swinton. By this time, he had earned the nickname Assface. He would chat and obviously flirt with me two, three times a day to all hours of the night, but with no follow-through.

He never once visited me in college at University of California Irvine. But I visited him at least a dozen times at USC. Maybe that was the problem. I gave in too easily. I was always willing to drive out to see him at the mention of hanging out. He, on the other hand, always had an excuse not to come over, or for me to go instead.

To his credit, he did visit me at home, with my parents, a few times. Those few visits kept me hoping and gave me assurance that he was interested, that I just had to be patient. I kept telling myself, *Next year will be the year he asks me out.* I just kept making excuses for him.

Chapter 7

As he became more involved at USC with intramural sports, fraternity, student body, clubs, and girls, we began to grow apart. He liked thinking he was cool, and me, Lily, the studious, innocent girl who attended his rival school, wasn't cool enough to be a part of his physical life. So I settled for his virtual life. I lived for those few increasingly sparse, yet captivating, online chats.

> Me: How was snowboarding?
> Carter: I brought back snow so you could see what it's like, but it melted…so sorry. I was like, I wish I could do this to your heart.
> Me: You're such a sweet talker
> Carter: So what if the sweet talk is the truth just said more candy like
>
> Me: Where do I fit into your life?
> Carter: You're the angel on my shoulder. Sometimes I ask myself what would Lily do?

Carter: What do I do? The girl I'm dating isn't happy with me. You always give good advice and you're a good honest person.

Carter: My girlfriend left me.
Me: Sorry to hear that.
Carter: I'm free to hang out. I miss you. Come over.

As our college years went by, I noticed the patterns Carter and I would fall into. I was a wonderful flirt buddy, his angel, his counselor, his confidante, his rebound. But never the girl of his dreams. And I was okay with that just as long as Carter was in my life. I figured it couldn't be too much longer before I made the leap from friend to girlfriend.

We both graduated, neither one of us attending each other's ceremonies. God didn't want our paths to cross, but I continued to find ways for them to diverge into each other.

The summer after graduation, I stepped up my game. I *called* Carter instead of instant messaging him, "We've never been out to dinner together. Invite me over and spend time with me." Surprisingly, he agreed, "Okay, how about sushi Thursday night? Come to my place, and I'll take us." He didn't have to tell me twice.

Dinner was nice. We went back to his place where he had a task for me. I wrote out thank you cards to his family for graduation gifts. At the time, I was just thrilled to be near Carter. Quite frankly, I may have been used as I transcribed his thoughts onto the stationary. I wrote *all* the cards. The only redeeming factor was his comment before I went home, "We make a great team," as he high-fived me. That was enough to keep me going until the next time we got together.

Chapter 8

He went to Pepperdine for law school and I went to Azusa Pacific University for graduate school and my teaching credential, creating an even greater physical distance between us. Despite the distance, he remembered my birthday every year, the delicate string that fused us together. He made me feel special; he'd do a countdown to my birthday every year, call on my special day, and then check-in with me and debrief after my birthday. But, did we ever spend my birthday together? Nope!

On June 15, 2005, five years to the day since we met, I mustered up the courage to call Carter. I prepared what I would say and hoped for his voice mail because I was so nervous. Of course, he picked up the phone and threw off my plan.

> Carter: Hi
> Me: Oh, hi. I was expecting your voice mail.
> Carter: I can hang up and let you call again. I won't answer.
> Me: Haha *(nervous laughter)*. I was just calling to say that it's been exactly five years since we met. I can't believe we're still talking.

> Carter: Ha. Ya that's cool. *His apathetic answer followed by the silence was killing me.*
> Me: So, how are you? *trying to save the conversation*
> Carter: Fine, but I gotta go. We'll talk later. Bye.
> Me: Ok, bye

His lack of enthusiasm for our continued contact fell on me like a ton of bricks. Something had to change. At the age of 22, five years after meeting Carter, I had only been in one serious relationship. Not because of a lack of interest from boys, but because I felt like I was cheating on Carter when I went out on dates. I was loyal to a boy who had no clue what I sacrificed for him.

An era of serial dating began. Boys came in and out of my life. No one ever lasted because in the back of my mind, these guys were just for the meantime. Despite my conscious decision to make a change, I couldn't shake the notion that Carter would come for me. So, they never meant anything to me. I never committed one hundred percent. They were just helping me bide my time until Carter finally realized that I was the woman for him.

It never failed. Each guy wanted me to be the last girl he dated. I broke so many men's hearts all in the name of Carter Swinton. For that, I apologize. I was playing games with every single one of them.

Chapter 9

We continued our unhealthy relationship of haphazardly instant messaging that led to our roughly twice a year random meet ups. Our time spent together was quality, we'd be found glued to each other, the strongest magnetic pull, as if time had stood still, picking up right where we left off. It was hard not to believe we weren't inseparable. But the magic had to end, Carter disappearing, leaving me wanting more, but having to settle for the instant messages.

Carter was so comfortable with me, to the point that he couldn't discern where to draw conversation boundary lines. The sounding board that I was to him, I never had the heart to point out inappropriate conversation topics he brought up and also for fear of less interaction with him. But, one day, around Christmas of 2006, I snapped. Carter balled up the muddied boundary line and threw it in my face, leaving me covered in disgust.

> Carter: Remember Lauren?
> Me: No
> Carter: Oh, I thought I told you about her. We've been
> dating for a while now. I think this could get serious. I
> really like her.

Me: Okay

Carter: You look alike. She has brown eyes and curly hair
like you. And she's skinny like you. She's a teacher like
you and she works out a lot just like you. I met her at
camp, the same place you and I met. You would like her.
I would like her?! He's gone mad! Keep your cool Lily.

Me: So, you're pretty much dating me.

Carter: I mean, you're not the same person but I guess, ya.
I do wish she were a little more like you though. You
dress better.

Me: That's too bad, the dressing part. *Keep it light. Just get
through this conversation.*

As if it weren't enough that he mentioned her, he seemed to
get a kick out of describing her. Was I supposed to be happy that
he was dating my clone? Was he trying to tell me that he was
attracted to me but I was not good enough to date? Seriously,
what was the purpose in that? Was I supposed to be thrilled that
all the girls he dated could be in the same lineup as me?

I was drained. Something had to change, I know I said it
before, but this time, seven years after meeting Carter, I was
going to do something drastic. He was slowly picking away at
me, watching me deteriorate. I couldn't let him see my undoing
so I blocked him from instant messenger and I signed up for an
online dating service. I was ready to find someone who would
love me without all the games. 2007 was going to be Carter free.

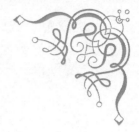

Chapter 10

Late January 2007, a few weeks into this novel endeavor, I met Rico Mayfield online. We started chatting on a Sunday morning into the late afternoon, so we decided to meet up for dinner. Mind you, we both had work the next day, and he lived an hour away, yet he was willing to meet up with me because he seemed to enjoy my company, already a drastic difference from Carter.

Physically, he didn't disappoint. He looked better in person. His online photos didn't do justice for his fierce green eyes and sparkling smile. He was an ultimate fighter (UFC) in ridiculously good shape. His muscular quads left no choice but for his jeans to hug his physique. Tribal tattoos wrapped around his equally impressive Herculean biceps, peeking out of his fitted white t-shirt. No doubt, he had washboard abs. A little superficial of me? Maybe.

Conversationally, I wasn't disappointed either. We had so much in common. He made me laugh, and most importantly, he made me forget about Assface, at least momentarily.

I was completely sold.

I pursued the relationship with Rico vigorously. But, somewhere deep in the reaches of my mind, something was gnawing at me, trying to breakout. I tried to shake the feeling without success. It would just have to be ignored.

I put my heart and soul into the relationship. Rico and I spent every weekend together, we travelled together, and we went to family functions together. I enjoyed his corny humor, and endearing idiosyncrasies, like flossing eight times a day. Rico treated me like a princess. In his eyes, I could do no wrong. We were falling in love. Carter was finally out of my life.

Then it happened one Friday night when Rico and I couldn't decide what movie to watch. I uncovered the source of my gnawing feeling.

After going through every aisle at Blockbuster, he settled on *Road Trip*. I panicked, slightly.

> Rico: Babe! What about *Road Trip*?
> Me: Ummm, no.
> Rico: What?! Why not? It's hilarious. Have you ever seen it?
> Me: Ummm, no.
> Rico: Then, it's perfect. I'm going to rent it for us.
> Me: Ummm, no.

I couldn't get any words out. I had a moment of unwanted clarity: Carter was back. I really thought I had a handle on my thoughts of Carter. His sudden reappearance scared me, made me feel defenseless.

Years ago, Carter mentioned that he wanted to watch *Road Trip* with me. I took that comment literally. So like a silly girl, I refused to watch it with anyone, even though I had many opportunities with friends. I was holding out to watch it for the first time with Carter Swinton. He has no idea what I sacrificed for him. Now, Rico was asking to watch that sacred movie with me.

I had two choices. I could either break through the barrier that kept me from truly becoming intimate with Rico and watch *Road Trip* with him or continue basking in the harsh rays of Carter's frivolous words.

I chose the latter, rationalizing my choice as an eccentricity. So I pushed through; I was going to prove to myself that I could function without Carter, that he wouldn't rule my life or my thoughts.

Despite my efforts, from that day on, in early May of 2007, the relationship between Rico and me started to dissipate. We constantly had petty arguments, wouldn't see eye to eye anymore, and even disagreed on how to spend our time together.

I needed to think. I needed to get away from everything I knew, sort out my feelings, and figure out my romantic life. I was confused. It was easier when all I did was obsess about Carter. Now I had thrown Rico into the mix, a situation that I had full control over. My solution: I applied for a two and a half month job as a camp counselor in a remote part of Greece.

Rico and I had the rest of May and a few weeks in June to say our goodbyes before I left for the summer. The plan was to take a break, no contact to give me my space, and wait for my return home with an answer, once I deliberated my thoughts and reenergized.

Five intense months after Rico and I met, I left for Greece. I'll never forget the look of despair in Rico's eyes when he dropped me off at the airport. I tried to focus on the fact that I was going to Greece, an exotic destination.

Chapter 11

Not knowing anyone, I arrived at the camp in Greece ready to battle my thoughts in solace. It was nice to know that no one knew my situation, leaving me to fend for myself without outside persuasion. How shocking it was that across the world, in a remote part of Greece, I stumbled upon two of Carter's cousins. *How could this be?!*

There were three times as many campers as the camp where I first met Carter, yet Alex's cabin of boys was paired up with my cabin of girls for activities, and Jackie was my camper. *Why, God, why? Was this a sign that I should be with Carter?*

While I physically got away from the drama back home, I was thrown right back into it a world away. Having to spend the entire two and a half months together, Alex and I became very good friends. I tried my best not to talk about Carter, but that was an epic fail. Alex did his best to give me advice, exactly what I didn't want to happen. The point of travelling across the world was to be as far removed from my situation as possible.

Jackie took an instant liking to me, without even knowing that I knew Carter. Once the secret was out, just like Nanette,

Carter's cousin who was my camper years ago, she proclaimed her love for me and wanted me to be a part of her family by marrying Carter. Unlike six year old, Nanette, she was seventeen, old enough to know exactly what she was talking about. I couldn't help but smile. *Why is it that everyone was rooting for Carter and me except for Carter?*

Meanwhile, Rico was *not* giving me the space we agreed I needed. I received countless e-mails from him professing his love for me. I so badly wanted to love Rico as passionately as he loved me. I really put myself between a rock and a hard place. Feelings should not be toyed with. Of all people, I should know this best.

All Carter ever did was side swipe my feelings, feeding my resentment for him. Now, I was doing the same exact thing to Rico. From the very beginning, my gut urged me to stay away from Rico, that I wasn't ready to completely commit to anyone. The summer that was supposed to be dedicated to reenergizing and rejuvenating myself, turned into a summer of horrific deliberating.

On the one hand, I was barraged with romantic e-mails from Rico, and on the other hand, showered with questions about my relationship with Carter. I couldn't make my mind stop running. As the summer was coming to an end, I was still no closer to figuring out what I wanted.

When I returned home in September, I felt so bad about having the slightest inkling of reservation about my love for Rico, this man who loved me beyond a doubt, that I continued the relationship, and with more fervor.

I really tried to make an effort to make it work. But as you know, if your heart isn't in something one hundred percent, it's impossible to be effective in the long term. I knew all the right things to say (thank you, Assface) and when to say them, but I knew that I couldn't put on this façade for much longer.

I loved Rico. I did. I still do. But, love doesn't conquer all. Fairytales lied to me. There's love, and then there's life. And most relationships are life.

While I was, once again, formulating a plan to step out of our mismatched relationship, I underestimated Rico's unconditional love for me. Rico brought up marriage and while I could picture marrying him, it wasn't the ideal life I imagined for myself.

January 2008, our one year anniversary, arrived way too soon. I was falling more in love with Rico while I was simultaneously falling out of love with him. One moment we'd get along so well, and the next moment we'd be fighting like cats and dogs. In the midst of all those emotions, thoughts of Carter haunted me, grazing my arms with icy fingers.

I did the unthinkable. I unblocked Carter from instant messenger early February 2008, more than a year from when I initially blocked him. He was online and immediately messaged me.

> Carter: Hi!!! Where have you been? I missed seeing you
>   online.
> Me: I've been around
> Carter: I was so excited when I saw you come online.

I'm glad you're here because I need your prayers for my surgery next week. When you pray, good things happen.

He turned up the volume on the charm and reeled me in, *again*. Not once did I question the fact that he missed me but never tried to call me over the past year. I was just ecstatic that he was contacting me at all.

I tried not to let the old habits resurface, yet I found myself drawn to his empty charm. I vowed to be the first to end the conversation, something I had trouble with a year prior. That was an unsuccessful endeavor. I missed him so much. Everything I felt in our brief online conversation was tantamount to my feelings for Rico. I had to end the relationship with Rico before I hurt him anymore.

Meanwhile, unbeknownst to me, Rico had big plans for us. Ironically, the day I chose to break his heart was the same day he chose to get down on one knee and propose to me. I froze. I tried to be in the moment, to feel the desire, to want Rico, but all I felt was sadness.

I didn't want to admit it, but I knew that my lack of one hundred percent effort with Rico had *everything* to do with Carter Swinton. Even though I loved Rico beyond a reasonable doubt, it wasn't enough to spend the rest of my life with him as long as Carter crowded my thoughts.

I came to the unfortunate realization, that Rico, and every other boy in my life since meeting Carter, was just a distraction. I was just biding my time until Carter professed his infinite love for me.

Rico had become my best friend and that's why it was so difficult for me to let go of him. He knew me like no one else knew me, inside and out. He understood and appreciated my humor, and we always had a wonderful time together. Yes, we argued, but who doesn't?

I was truly upset with myself for giving up a man who loved me more than life itself and wouldn't think twice about offering me the world on a silver platter. I couldn't believe I was giving up a tangible love for an abstract pseudo love. But, I did. Look what you've done to me, Carter Swinton.

Chapter 12

I was what Albert Einstein would call insane; doing the same thing over and over and expecting different results. I talked to Carter online over and over, and each year expected him to see me in a different light.

My parents started worrying about my well-being. One moment, I'd be as high as Mt. Everest because Carter said, "I don't like it when I can't hear your little giggle," and the next moment I would be as low as a teenage boy's pants because Carter disappeared for a few days. I needed to get help.

Eight years into my roller-coaster of love, which at some point turned to worship for Assface, I went to counseling sessions. I went for three months. I thought I was making progress. Apparently, the therapist thought otherwise when she dropped the news that she could no longer help me.

> Therapist: Lily, we've covered a lot of ground the last few months.
> Me: Yes, we have.
> Therapist: Unfortunately, I can't help you if you don't want to help yourself.

Me: What do you mean? *Was I getting kicked out of counseling?*

Therapist: You're an extremely intelligent girl. You understand your issue, and you know what tools you can use to overcome it, but you adamantly choose not to move forward.

Me: *Silence. I'm completely shocked.*

Therapist: I'm sorry Lily, but I can only be of assistance to you if you want to help yourself, and I just don't see that happening.

Me: *Scowl on my face. I'm coming to counseling. Isn't that getting help?*

Therapist: *As if reading my mind.* Coming to therapy isn't enough. Going through the motions is meaningless if your heart isn't in it. You're like a Sunday churchgoer who thinks she's faithful because she makes time for God an hour a week. You're not mentally disturbed, which is where I would come in. You're fully aware of what's going on, and you don't have a skewed view of your situation with Carter. You know where you stand, but you refuse to believe it and also refuse to change that.

Me: I *am* trying.

Therapist: Only you know if you truly are. But, professionally, I just don't see it. The leopard stool full of Carter goodies has to go, Lily. You're putting him on a pedestal, equating him with a god, which means he can never do any wrong in your eyes. A healthy relationship is one of equals, not with lessers or subservients. Unless you willingly decide to make significant changes, our sessions are not productive.

Me: Okay. I understand, but I'm not ready to give up my Carter box.

Therapist: And that's fine. When you finally do, I'll be here. Until then, you have quite a bit of thinking to do. Remember, you are in control of you, not Carter.

With that, counseling was over. I never went back. I never got rid of the leopard stool filled with Carter memorabilia. I was going to hold on to it until the items inside became antiques.

Two years after counseling, I see that Carter is human and that he has many faults; but I love him just the same, and I still have that box. I never open it anymore. It's just comforting knowing that it's there full of Carter keepsakes. It's like owning your favorite movie but never watching it. You just like knowing that you have access to it whenever you want.

Chapter 13

2008 was filled with surprises: breaking up with Rico, reconnecting with Carter, going to counseling, and meeting Carter's parents.

Easter of 2008, the spring after my trip to Greece, I got a chance to meet Carter's parents at our church picnic. Ever since I met Carter eight years ago, I found myself suddenly running into him every Easter picnic, as if he popped up out of nowhere.

Hence, there was incessant planning that revolved around that occasion. Weeks before, I would try on outfits that would bring attention to me. I would try on short body-hugging dresses, skintight jeans with close-fitting tops, even fitted sweaters in case the weather was cold. With every outfit, I had to try on a deluge of shoes, ranging from sandals to wedges to heels and jewelry. I had to find the *perfect* outfit.

I was determined to be prepared so that the day of the picnic all I had to think about was getting myself to the event. The Easter picnic became my favorite occasion, an event where I was guaranteed to run into Carter.

I had met his parents on previous occasions, but I never really had a chance to converse with them. This Easter, Carter's parents were interested in hearing about my trip to Greece since they were planning a trip there in a few months.

His mom absolutely fell in love with me. The gleam in her eyes, her body language, how she constantly complimented me and mentioned how adorable I was gave it away. I was thrilled simply to have her admire me.

Not in my wildest dreams would I have imagined that her enthrallment with me would result in her giving me her address and phone number, telling me to call her by her first name, and asking me to visit her *any* time. *Is this for real? Do parents even do that?*

I knew she was thinking about me for her son. *Yes! His parents are on my side. All I need now is for him to jump onto my side. He's almost there, just a little more coaxing.* That's not how it works though. I wasn't supposed to be strategizing on how to get the man of my dreams. He was supposed to be coming after me.

I couldn't wait to tell Carter how much his mom adored me. After the surprisingly pleasant conversation with Carter's parents, he came over to me and disgustedly brought up the fact that he couldn't believe his *entire* family loved me.

So far I'd met Nanette, Eric, Alex, and Jackie, four of his cousins and his mom and dad. "Everyone meets you and falls in love with you. What are you doing to them?" I quizzically cocked my head to the side, parted my lips to defend myself, but nothing came out; I was too shocked to speak. *Don't you want your family to approve of me? Isn't this a good thing?* I didn't understand his seething.

It still didn't stop him from flirting with me. He makes my head spin.

Chapter 14

Vanished from my life once again until the guarantee of next Easter in 2009, I was plagued with moments of depression the rest of the year. *How can Carter forget about me so easily? Am I forgettable? Do I not deserve his attention?* The more I analyzed the situation, the angrier I became, until finally: *HE'S NOT HUMAN!* That was the only logical conclusion I could come up with.

A few days before Easter, my depression disappeared and turned into elation; I knew I was going to see Carter. As guaranteed, I did see Carter. But this Easter, he came with a pretty girl, not Lauren, but another girl who had a similar figure as mine. *Ugh! Why can't it ever go my way?* Just like that, my elation turned into dejection. My family joked around about me being bipolar. I thought it was cruel for them to laugh at my heartache.

Clearly sullen and woeful, Carter still approached me. "You haven't been online lately," was his greeting to me. Silently, I cheered for my victory. My joy meter was slowly being filled. *How sad that it came to this? A word from Assface and I'm jumping off the walls. Hmm. Maybe I am bipolar.* He noticed that I wasn't available online. In my mind, that meant I mattered to him.

He was sitting next to the look-alike girl, another one to add to the lineup, and I was across the table talking to his cousin when I got a text message. My phone was not on silent, and it was a special text tone that only played when I received texts from you-know-who.

I took my phone out, not knowing what to expect. Thank goodness I had my back to Carter when I read the text. My jaw dropped. The emanating heat from the fire spontaneously combusting in my mouth and nostrils melted away everyone around me. I was ready for a fight. There's no way any devoted boyfriend would have texted me what I was seeing with his girlfriend sitting right next to him.

"You look really great. I miss being close to you. I hope to see you soon."

On the one hand, these were the texts I lived for. I loved it when he said I looked nice or that he missed me. But on the other hand, I'm not a home-wrecker, so I couldn't act on it. Why did these comments come at the most inopportune moments? What was I supposed to do with that information? I was sure my pounding heart was the same pounding in my head.

He frustrated the living daylights out of me! I turned to look at Assface, deservedly named so, ready to give him the death glare, only to be met by his seductive blue eyes—eyes that screamed, *I want you.* I could always count on his eyes to tell me his true emotions.

All I could think was, *I want you too, Carter. Just tell me what I have to do to have you, and I'll do it. Enough of this game. We both want each other, so what's the problem? Note to self, get my blood pressure checked.*

I removed myself from Assface's vicinity. I couldn't take anymore, at least not today. That would be enough drama for anyone, but my drama always seemed to be taken a step too far.

The picnic area was only so big and I eventually had to pass by him. He approached me, with that swagger, the one that screams,

"I'm coming for you," and stops me dead in my tracks. With the almost non-existent communication we had today, I can't help but wonder what he was thinking when he spread his arms wide embracing me in an unforgettably intimate and heated hug.

As if that weren't enough, he let his fingers trace my spine and linger on my lower back as he sensually rubbed me, slowly inching dangerously close to the curviest part of my body. And all this in front of his family *and* his girlfriend.

As much as I wanted to enjoy being in his arms, the thought of being one of James Bond's (in this case, Carter Swinton's) dispensable women came to my mind. Then I remembered how each of these women's desires for Bond consumed them to the point of brazenness. Without exchanging any words, Carter and I expressed our deep desires for each other, completely in the open. All my cares of being judged flew into the wind.

Out of the corner of my eye, I caught a glimpse of his girlfriend burning a hole through me with her fuming gaze. I was a threat to her. Carter reluctantly released me when his girlfriend pierced through our magical moment. "It's time to go. Remember, we're spending the rest of the day with your family at their house," she said through gritted teeth. She was trying to play it cool, but she already blew her cover with her bad attitude.

She reached for Carter's hand, and to my surprise, he pushed it away as he seductively gazed into my eyes. He was no longer being surreptitious about the nature of our relationship. His girlfriend tried, once again, to interlace fingers with Carter, only to be met with a swat.

He unwillingly turned away as I watched the ridiculous scene play out in front of me: Carter's girlfriend trying frantically to claim his hand as he adamantly avoided contact. Meanwhile, I chuckled maniacally to myself about the sheer absurdity of our situation. I was going mad with elated confusion.

It was like Carter and I were star-crossed lovers who could never be at the right place at the right time. There was always some circumstance that kept us apart, not to mention how thoroughly confused I was each time I saw him. He caused me a lot of anxiety trying to interpret his every move. Actions like these always threw me off. I knew he felt something for me. I just didn't know what exactly it was he felt and when the feelings I wanted him to feel would surface, if ever.

Chapter 15

After that wild Easter incident, Carter didn't vanish into thin air, but our conversations were limited and our encounters, zero.

My birthday was quickly approaching in October and I fantasized spending it with him in the Bahamas, or Hawaii, or Fiji. The closest I got was him texting me a few days before my birthday, asking what my plans were, something he did every year. And every year, I reacted the same exact way: elated that he remembered. Just as I mustered up the courage to ask him to spend my birthday with me, he dropped the bomb, "I'll be in Hawaii with my family on your birthday." Well, half my fantasy came true: he was going to Hawaii.

My birthday came and almost went without hearing from Assface. The saying, "hope for the best and expect the worst," didn't exist in my mind. My problem was that I always *expected* the best and hoped for nothing else. I was miserable all day because I didn't hear from Carter.

Over the last nine years, he *never* missed wishing me a happy birthday. Shortly before midnight, I got a text from Carter wishing me a happy birthday. Afterthought or not, I was jumping for joy because this year was extra special for me; I got a happy birthday text while he was vacationing in another state.

A few days later, Carter returned from Hawaii and called me to ask how my birthday went. This was a highly anticipated ritual every year. I knew he'd contact me sometime before my birthday, on my birthday, and sometime after my birthday.

Every year, without fail, instead of the entire month of October becoming celebratory, it would be filled with anxiety. I never knew how far in advance he'd call, or what time of the day he'd wish me a happy birthday, or how long after my birthday he'd check in.

I most likely raised my blood pressure significantly by fretting over hearing from him, which led me to lose my temper over inconsequential topics of discussion, temper tantrums as my family dubbed them. Did some of my closest friends forget my birthday? Absolutely? Did I care? Not at all.

Thankfully, for my family members, he was right on cue every year. Again, instead of taking his actions for face value, I glorified them, placing too much meaning on them. *He must care about me. Why go to those lengths to show me that my birthday was important? I didn't even do that for him.* My thoughts would go on and on and on.

Chapter 16

The pattern was that Carter's conversations with me slowly trickled off after my birthday and resumed after seeing me at the Easter picnic. This year, 2009, was different. He texted me and called me regularly. I wasn't about to put my guard down yet, but something was in the air. I could feel it.

After discovering where he traveled to in Hawaii, I had an urge to plan a trip there as well. As a matter of fact, I wanted to have the same exact itinerary as Carter. Going to the exact locations where he'd been gave me the sense that we were together, at least in spirit.

I could imagine him and me side by side snorkeling in the clear water with sea turtles swimming by. The imagery was easier for me to create if I placed myself in the same exact place Carter had been. That was my logic. It made complete sense to me.

I managed to convince two of my male coworkers to join me on a clone of Carter's trip to Hawaii. They didn't have to know that though. I loved the fact that I was traveling with two males because that was about the only time Carter showed any emotion. It was jealousy. I didn't belong to him, but he felt entitled to me no matter how long our absences from each other's lives were.

By March of 2010, Carter had upped the ante on our flirting. I had no idea what I was in for. He was talking to me daily on instant messenger, just like old times. He'd flirt, and we would even have deep conversations about books that we both read. I was really starting to like this. I could definitely get used to this.

He started calling me and saying things with double entendres like—"I'm looking for my honey"—while he was at the grocery store. Or, "Baby, I want you to be happy" when there would be a crying baby but clearly meaning it for me. That's his style. Everything has to be read between the lines. He just can't be direct. And somehow, I find it endearing.

However, over the years, his evasiveness conditioned me to act in the same way. Our communication suffered because of that. We shoved our issues under many rugs. We had filth laden floors underneath our collection of rugs. We were getting better at avoiding issues than dealing with them. And although this was not my communication style in the least, I assumed (which was the bane of my existence) that the more similar I became to Carter, the more he'd appreciate me.

The reality was that I was digging myself into a very deep hole, so deep that when I finally realized where I was, I was already too far down to rescue myself. Instead of fighting to get to flat land, I fought to survive in the dark hole. It was easier not to change courses. I assumed (once again the bane of my existence) that someday Assface would change courses and I would then follow suit. That day never came. I just ended up covered in dirt.

The only benefit, and I mean only, was that I became wittier. I had to find a way to keep myself entertained and sane. But at the same time, I developed a cynical and vague style of communication, a stretch from the eloquent, demure, and sincere girl I was before.

I saw him a few times within the next few months, more times than I had ever seen him in a year. He started contacting me multiple times a day asking how my day was going and just being great. He started showing quite an interest in me.

He talked about marriage and having babies and what we would name our kids. He chose the name, Daring, for a boy. Typical Carter—still a child. But loving him as much as I do, I was willing to name our child Daring. We talked about how we would raise our kids. Whether we would tell them Santa Claus didn't exist or "lie" to them, as he called it, about Santa bringing presents. We didn't agree despite his reasoning.

When he was growing up, his family didn't have a fireplace with a chimney. As an observant child, he became suspicious when he heard that Santa came through the chimney since they didn't even have one. So his next thought was, *So Santa just comes through the front door? That's ridiculous.*

With his logic at a premature age, he discovered there was no Santa and was thoroughly disappointed. He didn't want to cause such disappointment for his children. *I don't know about that, Carter. We'll have to revisit that topic later. I think imagination is an imperative part of growing up.*

I should have known, as soon as he mentioned "no Santa Claus," that there were deeper rooted issues. Imagination is part of childhood. Withholding creativity from a child for the sake of correctness is selfish. Assface doesn't lack in that department. I don't know if there is any better adjective to describe him than selfish. His way or no way. And somehow, I wanted to be a part of his way and weasel my way in.

Clearly, his way lends itself to being closed-minded. Recalling past conversations, he aggrandizes his rationality. It's hyper-realism, which doesn't jive with many people, hence why he's constantly trying to defend one viewpoint or another. He's politically correct but only for his own viewpoints, which is quite contradictory.

Chapter 17

Even so, Carter and I remained on "dating" terms. We went out to eat together, watched movies, stargazed, and spent quality time together. At least, it's the closest to dating we ever got to. We saw each other often, talked on the phone more often, and chatted online even more often. Life was great; my dream was finally coming true. Carter and I were together. Feels like déjà vu. *Didn't I say those exact words a few years ago, and nothing came of us?*

Easter 2010 wasn't a light at the end of a tunnel, as it was each year. This time, I was blinded by the light; there was no tunnel. Just my birthday with a fast track to Easter. I planned a surfing trip to Costa Rica on my own and didn't quite check the dates. For the first time, I had to miss the Easter picnic, which meant no Carter.

The one year that I should have been at the Easter picnic, I missed it. Finally, the tides were on my side and I recklessly extended my vacation on a whim, not noticing that that day I flew back was Easter. I would be home just in time for the end of the picnic. I think it was a sign from God. He made our paths intentionally avoid each other. Yet, I still refused to believe that God's plan for me didn't include Carter Swinton.

In the rush of life, I forgot to mention to Carter that I was going to Costa Rica. When he eventually found out, he wasn't too happy with my disappearing act. I misconstrued that for care, when in reality, it was a control issue.

As long as I was under his thumb, we were on great terms. As soon as I took matters into my own hands, Carter and I would find ourselves on opposite ends of the world. The difference between us though, was that I was willing to work through any issue to be with him, while he ran away at the mere hint of a conflict.

So when my mom and my sister went to the picnic without me, he was confused. I told them to be my spies, and I specifically told my mom to tell only Eric, Carter's cousin, that I said hello. My mom did just that, but Carter was within earshot, and my sister laughed to herself at his expression. She said he looked quite upset that my mom didn't have a message to deliver to him.

As my mom and my sister walked away, Carter hurried over to them to talk. My mom said he was definitely trying to make a good impression on her and asking if I was there, and when she talked about me, his eyes lit up. I can't believe I missed this! The year 2010 is the only year I missed the picnic, and it's the only year we finally had some sort of *real* relationship.

Nonetheless, I was excited by his actions. This was finally going somewhere. My mom, being a mommy, said to me, "He was clearly trying to make a good impression, but so what? He isn't acting on it, and until then, don't hold your breath."

I didn't want to believe her. I dove headfirst into this development and didn't guard myself with any armor. After years of dealing with Carter, I should have known that he is fickle and nothing lasts.

Chapter 18

When I returned from my Costa Rica trip, things were great between us. *See mom, we're doing just fine.* His birthday is in May, and he actually invited me, for the first time, to hang out with his friends. In the ten years that we had known each other, I had never met his friends. This was a milestone. He never introduced me to his friends or ever told them that I exist. I was always the mystery girl.

We have mutual friends at church, and not a single one of them knew that we knew each other. On the one hand, the thrill of the secret was kind of exhilarating. Shy, naive girl gets to play with the hot jock, but no one would suspect. The only problem was that we weren't having an affair, for goodness sake. We just bounced back to each other every so often to have a good time. The novelty of the secrecy eventually expired; it had gone on far too long.

While in actuality it was Carter's birthday, I felt like I was the birthday girl, getting introduced to all his closest friends. Oddly enough, it didn't strike me as strange that he still introduced me as his friend and nothing more until I went home and analyzed the day. I was too wrapped up in finally meeting his other "family." Maybe my mom was right.

His birthday was a full day on the beach playing volleyball and goofing off and then going to a bar to watch the Lakers play basketball on the big screen TVs.

I arrived at the beach a few hours late; I didn't want to seem too eager. I showed up in my leopard bikini and laid out on my leopard towel. He went wild. He loved it. The entire afternoon, he gave me all kinds of attention. He would wave to me during his volleyball games or say things like, "Rawr, I love the leopard. Do you make the noises too?" all in front of his friends. He loves that I love leopard print.

In the past, he would try to impress me by wearing his leopard boxers whenever I came over to hang out. "I wore them just for you, Lily," he'd seductively say. My favorite was when he would text me pictures of leopard displays just to tell me he was thinking about me.

Later on, when the games ended and it was time to go to the bar, I opted to hang out on the beach to watch the sunset. That's more my style. He kept trying to convince me to hang out with his friends, but I refused, saying that I'd rather stay on the beach and enjoy the scenery.

The entire time he was at the bar, he was texting me. "First quarter is over. Only three more minutes until the fourth quarter is over. Don't leave until I get to hang out with you. The UFC fight is on. Don't you want to come watch it?" He missed me. So I stayed at the beach until he came back.

In retrospect, I should have gone with him to the bar to spend more time with his friends. While I was trying to prove to myself that he enjoyed my company and wanted me around, he was most likely irritated and possibly even embarrassed that the girl he liked was being antisocial.

Though this story is about me and my feelings, it's important to note this particular incident because it shows Carter's true fickle identity. If I don't fit in with the trend or act in a precise manner, he has second thoughts about me.

"I left early, you know, so that I could come see you," he said, as if I should be impressed. If we were truly an item, he should have stayed with me at the beach. But I brushed it off when he redeemed himself by ordering food for me when he heard my stomach rumble. He remembered that I don't like tomatoes, onions, lettuce, and bell peppers, which I thought was awesome.

The stickiness from spending all day at the beach was getting to me; I needed to take a shower. "Look at it," as he pointed to the towel he brought for me.

I was overwhelmed by his sweetness. The towel had a ballerina on it. He knows that I dance ballet. So thoughtful. I didn't want the night to end, but of course it did, and in such an unpleasant way. His friends kept texting him to come out to another bar to hang out.

He kept telling them that he was hanging out with me. But finally, he gave in and asked me if he could go. What was I supposed to do? Tell him no? So I said that's fine.

Sadly, he didn't invite me to go along. I didn't know it then, but that was the peak of our relationship. That was the highlight. That's it. From there, everything went downhill. I was at the highest point in my life because of a stupid boy, not because of God.

If I were thinking rationally, which never seemed to happen in Carter's presence, the day should have unfolded much differently. First, I should have received a phone call when I didn't arrive anywhere near on time. His lack of concern for my safety should have been a red flag. Second, I should have been introduced as his girlfriend or simply Lily, without a title at all. Third, whether he wanted to watch the basketball game or not, he should have stayed with me on the beach or at least found a way to convince me to join him at the bar. Fourth, Carter should have spent the rest of the evening with me instead of leaving to meet his friends or he could have taken me with him.

If I had taken a moment to even briefly inspect the day with my naked eye, no microscope necessary to witness Assface's self-regard, I would have easily detected his insincerity and disrespect. What's the common thread between all his actions? Selfish, selfish, selfish, and more selfish. There was no consideration for Lily anywhere during the entire day.

Students in school have state testing and are scored based on their skills with a scale, the lowest being far below basic all the way up to advanced. The way Assface treated me wouldn't even have a score. He was even lower than far below basic in dating capacity.

Chapter 19

A few weeks after Carter's birthday, at the end of May, I left for Israel. He called me before I left. "I don't think I can get through the week with you gone," he thoughtfully said. How sweet. I suddenly wanted to cancel my trip to Israel to stay with Carter.

Once again, I didn't immediately pick up on the empty charm. Words! That's all they were! Blindly living my life in a fairytale was going to take a toll on my sanity, as I later found out.

I traveled with a few friends from out of state, whom I hadn't seen in a while, and they noticed that I was unusually cheerful. What came out of my mouth when I tried to explain my joy was ridiculous. I was on cloud nine, and nothing could bring me down. "I'm getting married next year! Carter and I are finally serious!" Their confused looks saddened me until someone asked, "Who's Carter?"

I forgot that most of my friends didn't know Carter by any name other than Assface, and rightfully so. Most of my experiences with him were unpleasant. Why I was still in love with someone nicknamed Assface and who was known by all my friends by the same name was baffling.

When I got back from Israel, he picked me up from the airport—because I asked him to—and took me to his house, where we hung out for an hour or so. My sister picked me up from his house, a few minutes away from the airport.

He couldn't even take me all the way home. He didn't want to. Stupid me. That was a sure sign that he didn't care all that much for me. I would have dropped everything, or even woken up early or stayed up late if he needed a ride home from the airport.

This was the last time I saw him.

Over the next few days, Carter's texts became more sporadic and didn't carry the same enthusiasm as before. Something was wrong. I knew that it had to be some other girl or that he was losing interest for some reason, but I didn't want to believe it. I tried to continue to keep up the texting and the cuteness, but he just wasn't having it. And there the great cloud of sadness arrived, and remained.

50 Crazy Things I've Done

1. Singing romantic songs to his picture
2. Picking up the lanyard he dropped at camp and gluing it in my Carter notebook
3. Having a leopard box full of Carter memorabilia
4. Having a notebook filled with highlighted instant message conversations
5. Drawing pictures of him on children's menus at restaurants and while working as a preschool aide during art time
6. Staying up all night just for the chance that he might come online and chat with me
7. Switching calls using call waiting, thinking it was him, but really my same friend just calling me from her landline rather than her cell phone, putting on my sexy Carter voice

8. Seeing a Subaru Impreza and getting excited, every time (it's what he drives)
9. Blowing off my boyfriend to see Carter instead
10. Responding to his texts or instant messages only after I've run my response by a few friends
11. Consciously thinking about him and staring at the framed picture of Carter and me before going to bed in an attempt to dream about him (the photograph was never removed from my desk throughout the entire ten years)
12. Going to the same places he's gone simply to tell him we do the same activities
13. Looking at his Facebook multiple times a day
14. Posting up pictures and statuses on Facebook geared for him, in hopes that he would comment
15. Going over to his house at 3 or 4 a.m. on a work night just to spend even an hour or so with him
16. Making up and embellishing my stories so that I can look good to him (if he went horseback riding, then I went moonlight beach horseback riding)
17. Calling him my boyfriend to everyone even when we weren't dating
18. Writing a book about him
19. Practicing what jokes I would say to him so I would sound funny
20. Going to USC parties just on the off chance of running into him
21. Making excuses for all his bad behavior
22. Buying the same CD that he let me borrow
23. Finding out what music he likes and saying I liked it too
24. Making my friend create a fake online identity in order to talk to him and find out information about him
25. Researching his favorite sports players, music, and interests so that I could have some commentary on them, as if I knew everything

26. Never disagreeing with him
27. Always picking up the phone and responding immediately, no matter the time of day or night
28. Using his first and last name in word problems in math books I wrote for work (these are published)
29. Being mad at any friend who had an event the same time that Carter invited me anywhere
30. Getting so excited every time Carter called that I would jump up and down and scream
31. Going on a shopping spree at the thought of spending time with him and buying clothes that he would love
32. Buying a tennis racket and tennis balls because he got into tennis and suggested that he would teach me (he never did, and the racket and balls are still in the packaging)
33. Taking the day off work without telling him, without knowing if he would be home, and going to the beach by his house, hoping that I would run into him
34. Cleaning my room every time he came over so he would never suspect that I'm disorganized or messy
35. "Accidentally" calling and texting him just to see how he would respond
36. Telling him that I was dating when I really wasn't, just to get a reaction from him
37. Having a list of all the girls he dated so I can cross off each girl as soon as I find out she is married through Facebook (one less potential girl to get back together with means I'm closer to the top)
38. Buying very expensive tickets off eBay to go to a USC/ UCLA football game in hopes of running into him (it was the only year he decided not to go)
39. Keeping a list of all his addresses from childhood to present
40. Sharing every online conversation and every text to friends to help me analyze what Carter "really" meant

41. Going to a Reiki master to help me cut the cord, and all she could say was that Carter has a strong psychological hold on me that would be difficult to disconnect

42. Using his screen name and birthday for all my passwords and pin numbers

43. Kissing him before I kissed my boyfriend (I was holding out so that I could say Carter was my first kiss)

44. Calling his mom from time to time without him knowing so that I could have lunch with her on the off chance that she would bring me up in conversation with him at a later time

45. Telling Carter's little cousin to convince him that he should marry me because she wanted me to be a part of the family

46. Going to therapy to try to get over Carter and ending up getting kicked out because the counselor said I already knew how to fix the problem but didn't want to take any further action

47. Recording every voice mail I got from Carter onto a cassette tape so I could listen to his voice

48. Having conversations out loud with imaginary Carter while I was walking to class in college

49. Highlighting all the days Carter contacted me in a calendar, trying to find a pattern

50. Writing his name on the dust on my laptop screen and the steam on my glass shower door so that at just the right angle Carter is always seen

As a way to cope with my sadness, I started journaling shortly after my return from Israel.

Wednesday, June 9, 2010

Walking down Morado Road on my lunch break, I called Carter to tell him a funny story. I called because everyone loves a little levity in their day.

"You would not believe what I did today. My student must think I know nothing about street life. His watch was beeping, distracting the rest of the class, and he wasn't doing anything about it. Oddly enough, he was wearing it on his ankle. Irritated, I snapped at him to turn off his anklet watch. He just started laughing at me," I casually explained.

"Miss, I'm on house arrest. I've passed the time limit to be a certain distance from my home. I can't turn it off, even if I wanted to."

I chuckled at myself even as I was telling Carter my silly story. Here I was working in a high school full of juvenile delinquents and I had no idea what a house arrest device looked like. There went my credibility.

Carter didn't find my story funny. I was met with a deafening silence. No reaction.

Instead, I was brutally clobbered with, "I've been thinking for a long time about us, and I don't think we are compatible." Then the flash of lightning struck; "I met someone who is more about me than you are right now." *What does that even mean?? How do you go from talking about marriage and babies to nothing at all??*

In one fleeting moment, all two months of what we shared was gone, as if it never happened. Thirty-five minutes later, the call that was supposed to make Carter laugh made me hurt.

I didn't cry. Immediately after hanging up, I felt like I was having a heart attack, at least the way I imagined what a heart attack felt like. My heart was literally being attacked to brokenness. The pounding of my heart made it feel as if it were bigger than my chest, about to burst into a million little pieces.

I genuinely thought my heart was shattering and that I wouldn't be able to piece it back together. Even if I could, it would be eternally scarred and extremely fragile from all the cracks.

Look what you've done to me, Carter Swinton.

Thursday, June 10, 2010

I didn't know whether to cry or laugh or scream. I woke up confused after a vivid dream where Carter and I were hanging out and having a good time.

> The Dream: Out of nowhere, an obese girl with a unibrow walked by, Carter lost focus, and I completely lost control of our conversation. I followed his gaze, only to find him ogling this *thing*! He got up without a word to me, grabbed her hand, and walked away. My shock was unconcealable, evident in my dropped jaw. It's as if this *thing* had a hold over him. He was clearly in love.

As a disclaimer, I have nothing against heavier people or those who choose to keep their eyebrows thick. However, I know that I was the better-looking one in my dream.

Do I dare try to interpret the dream? I felt defeated in every way shape and form. Not a good start to my day.

The settling storm cloud seemed all too comfortable suspended over my head, taunting me with its morose streaks of gray to feel even worse today than yesterday.

I cried at work to my coworkers Maggie and Yvonne. Even with such great support all around me, I couldn't shake my sadness.

Inspirational quotes kept flooding my e-mail inbox. Instead of making me feel better, they made me feel worse. *Crazy Lily can't get over Carter, can't let go of someone undeserving of her.*

Just because a friendship or relationship ends does not mean that the other person is a bad person. Nor does it mean that the other person is crazy. Nor does it mean that the other person never cared about you or any of those things we often say. It simply means that it wasn't meant to work out and though it is horrible and unfortunate and sometimes heartbreaking, it's not the end of the world. Other friends will come along, other boyfriends and girlfriends will come along. Sometimes things just aren't meant to be. And that has to be okay. It has to be okay because otherwise what do we have?

Eventually one of two things will happen: He'll realize you're worth it or you'll realize he isn't.

You'll never find the right person, if you can't let go of the wrong one.

I guess it's gonna have to hurt, I guess I'm gonna have to cry; and let go of some things I've loved, to get to the other side. I guess it's gonna break me down, like falling when you try to fly; it's sad, but sometimes moving on with the rest of your life, starts with goodbye.

I don't know what you are going through and I don't need to know. I just wanted to say that you are an amazing teacher and the kids love you. The second thing I wanted to say is that God loves you as well.

"For I know the plans I have for you," declares the Lord, "plans to prosper you and not to harm you, plans to give you hope and a future" (Jeremiah 29:11).

The reminder of God's plans for me satiated my sadness momentarily.

After the day that never seemed to end at work, I went to my private ballet lesson and my private voice lesson. I've always been told you're not supposed to give up your routine to sulk, so it was business as usual.

Instead of dancing, I cried in front of April during my ballet lesson. There was no ballet tonight, only April politely listening to my "dumping" story. Can you believe it? She had something positive to say about the situation, a silver lining, which also made me feel more sorry for myself. *Why can't I accept my situation?*

"Lily, all I can think after hearing all this is that you are one lucky bitch. If Brandon dumped me that nicely, I would be so happy. You're lucky he was that nice and upfront with you. He didn't have to be." Wow, she's right. I'm the luckiest girl alive. (Note the facetiousness).

After not dancing and not feeling better about my situation, I went to my voice lesson. Instead of singing, I cried in front of Nora. Nora wasn't having it. "I really am sorry about your situation, but you're here to sing. Why not pick an uplifting song."

I started singing *Here I Am To Worship*, a praise song. With every line I sang, more tears poured out, while the storm cloud simultaneously dissipated. This time the tears were coming from a place of realization, of a want and need to change the direction of my life.

While I was coming to terms with my life, while singing completely out of tune, with intermittent sobs, tears streaming down my face, I saw Nora stifling laughter. Guaranteed she's never given a voice lesson like this before.

I was at a full blown sob now. Right then and there, I realized that I need to give my problems to God and stop trying to take the reins on my life.

Faith is taking the first step, even when you don't see the whole staircase. I know there is a plan for me somewhere out there. I just need to relax and let God do His job instead of taking it away from Him.

Friday, June 11, 2010

I felt great and liberated and rejuvenated today. I had no more responsibilities in my love life. God willingly took over for me when I handed him the ropes yesterday. I haven't shed a single tear. There's no need for me to be upset over someone who doesn't care about me as much as I care about him.

I put on a floral summer dress, matched it with gold sandals and a gold headband, and went to work in a relieved mood, now that the storm cloud was gone.

In the midst of my crisis, I forgot that today was an important day at work. I, along with a few coworkers were hand-picked to have lunch with the owner of the school where I work.

This is why I believe in God. It's no coincidence that my voice lesson was last night, and that my perspective on my situation changed just in time for me to pick up my broken pieces and look presentable for this lunch meeting.

Out of formality, he asked each of us about our lives and how we're doing. A few people answered with customary responses: "I'm well. Family is healthy. Life is good." While others responded with sycophant comments: "I love my job. I couldn't be happier."

I, instead, blurted out, "I just broke up with my boyfriend." Why I said that is ludicrous and beyond me. It just came out. I felt like I had Tourette's. First of all, he wasn't even my boyfriend, at least not by title. Second of all, this was the first time I met Jared Hart; I had no previous relationship with him to give him insight into my personal life.

The most comical part of my comment was that a few coworkers turned to me and mouthed, "Assface?" I must have told the entire universe about Carter Swinton.

Jared's genuine concern when he asked if I needed a few days off from work was accompanied by stifled laughter from my coworkers. Once again, I'd managed to blow my situation out of proportion and I struggled to keep myself from bursting into laughter.

The rest of lunch went well, with no more interjections about my personal life.

I felt good. I managed to bring levity to the table through my "crisis" and more importantly, I didn't get fired from my job for being unprofessional at a work meeting.

Of course, when I feel greatest is when temptation comes knocking at my door.

I walked in the front door, and turned on my computer, out of habit, even before putting my purse down. I checked my Gmail and instantly, who other than "the problem" IMed me on Gchat, commented on one of my Facebook pictures, and tried to be friendly.

    Carter: u look ripped in that pic

So now I'm confused. Why did he just IM me? He just told me two days ago he didn't want to be with me. Now I'm just supposed to be his friend with no repercussions for him but every emotional roller-coaster for me? This isn't a fair deal at all.

Then, I remembered a basic principle of attraction: my distance combined with the appearance that I had self-control was making him nervous. (He thought he might lose me).

I didn't cry during our last phone call a few days ago, and he had no clue what I went through the few days afterward. It took all the power I had to get off the phone calmly while the storm brewed in my heart and mind on Wednesday. A happy thought entered my mind: maybe he was coming back for me.

There are just too many ways to communicate. Even if I wanted him out of my life, I'm connected in too many indirect ways. I would have to change my identity in order for him to be disconnected from me.

I felt like Drew Barrymore when she vents her frustration about technology in *He's Just Not That Into You*. She was trying to connect with a guy whose schedule just didn't jive with hers. After he left her a voice mail at her work, she called his home, he e-mailed her, she texted him, and it got frustrating. In the end, she was rejected by seven different technologies.

Although Carter isn't pursuing me per se, he has access to me in too many ways, where he doesn't even have to think about consequences. When he contacts me with a particular portal of technology, I question his choice. I drive myself nuts trying to consider his choice.

Saturday, June 12, 2010

I finally had a day all to myself to relax and just enjoy doing nothing. However, this wasn't the time I wanted it. Carter's short, most likely meaningless comment to me yesterday kept my mind and tear ducts on overdrive.

None of the invitations to go out today sounded exciting, so I spontaneously bought a new mattress for my twin size, "kindergarten" bed, as Carter called it, to try to get out of my funk. But, even the mundane task of buying a new mattress had a connection to Carter. Everything I do, see, or touch can somehow be connected to that man who drives me crazy.

"Hello Ma'am. What kind of mattress can I help you find?" asked the salesman. Before I could answer, my subconscious shoved my tongue aside and took over the words coming out of my mouth.

"Long story short, I thought I was going to be married, and now I'm not. I thought I was going to be getting a mattress with my husband." As soon as I uttered the words, even I knew I had gone too far. Compulsive lying, or as I like to call it, compulsive imagining, is just way too easy for me.

My imagination had sprung to life. Trouble. That's what my daydreams had become. I was living in my dreams. I existed in the perception of a future that had never happened.

These days, my unconventional responses to questions elicited facial expressions unfamiliar to me. I've never been that person to bring confusion or dismay to someone else's face. I've always brought happiness and laughter to others.

Sunday, June 13, 2010

I didn't go to church. God wasn't particularly inspiring to me today. *I'm sorry God, I know you should always be number one, especially when I'm feeling low, but I'm feeling too blah, if that's even an emotion.*

I did nothing but sulk today until a friend took me to Starbucks to cheer me up with her brilliant idea. "I figured it out Lily. Here's all you have to do to forget about Assface. I learned this trick in psychology class. Wear a rubber band around your wrist, and every time you think of Carter, snap the rubber band to condition yourself out of your Carter thoughts."

I was desperate enough to push my skepticism aside and try it.

Monday, June 14, 2010

I was no longer sad. I was angry! Why was this asshole impacting my life so much? Why was he making me feel sick to my stomach? All day long, the rubber band was being snapped. Was there anything on my brain besides this fool? *I miss Carter.* Snap. *Why did Carter leave me?* Snap. *When will I stop thinking about Carter?* Snap. By the end of the day, it looked like I had tried slitting my wrist.

After work, my friend Yvonne and I went to the beach— Manhattan Beach—of course, where Carter lives. We found parking a block away from his house. I had mixed feelings about potentially seeing him. Initially, I so badly wanted to "accidentally" run into him. But when I didn't, I thanked God for that small blessing.

What happened instead was Yvonne talked some sense into me and gave me a beating with her words. I came to some great realizations with her help and decided to start anew, Carterless.

"Lily! There's so much for you to focus on. You're shopping for your first home, all by yourself. Start thinking about how you want to furnish it. That's a brand new life right there. Why dwell on Assface, who by the way, I've never met and I'm your best friend. What does that show you about him? He wasn't around enough."

Not even Yvonne's pep talk could prepare me for the emotions that coursed through my veins during the drive home from Manhattan Beach. Every turn, a memory of Carter magically materialized. I couldn't look any direction without his image emerging from thin air, as if the curtain was just pulled back the second I glanced up. I wondered why I hadn't noticed on the drive to the beach.

Just driving through Manhattan Beach, I saw Carter and myself sitting together at each café where we shared meals together. Driving down the 110 freeway, we passed by USC, his alma mater. Every memory of us spending time on campus with each other flashed before my eyes. The day I showed up to his dorm wearing hot pink leather shorts and cornrows in my hair, the day we were in a rush to get out of the rain and got a parking ticket, the day we ordered seasonal drinks from Starbucks that we both didn't like. The memories continued flooding my mind.

A little farther down on the 5 freeway, we passed by his high school and the exit for his home when he lived in Burbank. The first time I saw him outside of camp was here in his backyard.

On the 2 freeway, we passed by the exit for his Glendale home. (His family moved often and I visited every home and have memories attached to each one). An image of us innocently kissing as his parents pulled into the driveway and both of us trying to act as if nothing happened brought a flicker of a smile to my face.

Every freeway had a landmark that made it impossible to ignore the presence of Carter in my life. Even if I wanted to forget him, I couldn't. There were too many reminders surrounding me.

Tuesday, June 15, 2010

Going down memory lane must have flushed some of my negative feelings out because I was in a great mood, ready for a new start, feeling awesome. Nothing, and especially no one, could bring me down.

Wednesday, June 16, 2010

Wouldn't you know it, a dream brought me down. Fresh starts are always accompanied by a stroke of bad luck. Today was just that day. As if it wasn't enough that he was on my mind every waking second, he was apparently on my mind every sleeping second as well.

I woke up sad, sad, sad. Carter got married in my dream, unfortunately, to a really nice girl, whom I liked. He took me aside and told me he was sorry we didn't work out, that I will always be very special to him, and that he will always care about me very much.

I knew it wasn't real but this mirrored how I felt in reality. I don't want to like who he marries. I don't want anyone to bring him that kind of happiness, unless it's me.

Remember those dreams when you are wetting your pants in public only to wake up realizing you're wetting your pants for real? I think I would rather have woken up to that than to crying about Carter. He's totally overtaken my life. What an intrusion!

Thursday, June 17, 2010

Really? More dreams? Enough already!

Carter and I are lying in bed with three other girls, including my sister, sleeping on either side of us. We decide to fool around nonetheless. Shortly after, everyone wakes up and hasn't a clue what happened. Come on! How is it possible for three other people to be completely oblivious to that kind of action inches away from them?

My relationships with Carter were always a secret in my dreams. Why am I not worthy enough to share with the rest of his world? This scared me. Wasn't that the reality of our situation? I'm too scared he won't include me in his life, but I'm also too scared he won't include me in his life the way *I* want to be included.

It was just a dream, but it led me to a day of pondering and sadness, with tears interspersed throughout. *God, where are you?*

Friday, June 18, 2010

The company picnic was an ideal setting for Lily, master storyteller. I don't even know how much of my stories are true anymore. I embellish them so much. I can't differentiate if I do this for shock value to evoke a reaction from people or because my exaggerated stories validate my actions, at least in my mind.

"Hey Lily, I heard you've been having a rough time. Are you doing okay?" asked a coworker.

"Thanks for asking." As if on cue, my eyes started tearing up. "It's been rough. My boyfriend, Carter, and I had been together for ten years off and on. Shortly after we talked about getting married and having babies together, he vehemently dumped me for another girl."

I sighed loudly, paused for effect, and took a look at the crowd that gathered to hear my story. I believably composed myself and continued.

After my long-winded explanation for what really didn't happen, I was showered with looks of sympathy and warm hugs.

If I could tell the true story, Carter and I have known each other for ten years and we've spoken off and on throughout the years. We've dabbled in dating almost never and talked about marriage and babies in fun. In reality, he was bound to meet another girl, since we never defined our relationship, even those last two amazing months together. We were always in limbo.

The realization today: *I'm pathetic for letting this fool turn me into a liar.* Even though I have full control over what I said, I still blame him for my verbal transformations.

Realization number two: I need to go back to counseling.

Saturday, June 19, 2010

To the day's credit, it started off well. I had a masseuse come over and de-stress me for an hour and a half. Instead of having a clear mind, I thought about none other than Carter Swinton.

Shortly after, I viewed a townhouse in Monrovia with my realtor and put an offer on it. Maybe this is what I need—a fresh new start with something of my very own to keep my mind off other things, like stupid boys.

Later that night, I went to an Imogen Heap concert with my sister and my friend, and all I could think was, *Carter would like this.* So many missed opportunities together. Ugh! Ugh! Ugh!

Sunday, June 20, 2010

I'm angry again. Make up your mind, Lily. I woke up to the thought of running into Carter next year at the Easter picnic, the only place I'm almost guaranteed to run into him, and giving him a piece of my mind. What's the point a year later? I should already be over him by then. Right?

I tried to channel my anger by calling everyone I knew who would be willing to listen to my Carter stories.

Monday, June 21, 2010

I woke up sick. I stayed in bed and read, *The Shack*, a Christian book that Carter lent me. It was amazing. It did wonders for me.

I want God in my life so badly. This book gave me more answers to questions about religion than any book or priest had managed to give me. I wonder why Carter gave it to me to read, saying it's a good book, when he himself doesn't even believe in God and religion. What irony Carter brings to my life.

Today was also the first time I saw Carter online since Friday, June 11. I thought for sure he was blocking me. Then, I thought, I analyze way too much.

I wanted to message him, but then I remembered wise words: anything a person chases in life runs away. Not that I had him to begin with but I didn't want him to run even farther away.

Tuesday, June 22, 2010

I was supposed to go to the beach with my friend today. Can you guess what beach? That's right. Manhattan Beach, Carter's beach.

I stayed home and rested since I was sick with the flu. I suppose you could argue that I'm sick in the head with all this Carter Swinton madness, but that's all relative depending on who you ask. And if you ask me, I'm not sick in the head; I just philosophize.

I kept reading *The Shack*. It's miraculous. It made me feel calm and peace in my life. For once, since that frightful Wednesday, thirteen days ago, I felt tranquility. I felt light and feathery, like a burden had been lifted off my shoulders. I wanted to feel like this every day.

I realized that I can, but I have to give *everything* to God. He is in control, not me. I never was and never will be. The illusion that I gave myself took me too many steps backward in this game of life. But, it's only a game when I try and take over. It's real life when I let God lead me and live within me.

All I have control over is today and nothing more. The rest is up to God. There's a story that my priest told me once about letting go and trusting God. It came to mind now.

There was a man holding on to a tree branch for dear life. He called out, "Help! Is anyone out there?"

A booming voice from nowhere and everywhere answered, "I'm here."

The man asked, "Who are you?"

"I am God."

"Okay, can you please help me?"

God replied, "Yes, just do as I say."

"I'll do anything! Just help me."

"Let go of the tree branch," God calmly instructed.

The man shuddered at the thought and asked, "Uh, is there anyone else out there?"

The toughest part is the beginning—letting go and trusting that the Lord will protect you and only has your best interests in mind.

Wednesday, June 23, 2010

What a ridiculous day! Everything that happened today was a fluke. Everything!

I had the day off and decided to go to Manhattan Beach. I like Manhattan Beach. I really do. There might be a slight chance that I like it more because Carter lives there.

My rationalization for choosing that beach is that I've been to Carter's place often enough; I can just drive there on autopilot. I can navigate the area, and I know all the secret spots for parking.

I figured I'd return his book, *The Shack*, since I was trying to flush out anything Carter in my life. For sure, I thought coming on a weekday would guarantee zero run-in with Carter since he should be at work.

I parked my car and eagerly walked to Carter's house ready to purge him from my life, as if leaving the book on his front doorstep would instantly make my gray skies blue.

This was the end. No more ties to Carter.

In my life, nothing goes as planned. As I neared his house and recognized the familiar white rear bumper of his Subaru Impreza peeking out of his garage, my heart jumped out of my chest. *Oh, for goodness sake! It's Wednesday. Why isn't he at work? He never takes a day off.*

Not backing down from my mission, I snuck up to his doorstep and left the book at the foot of his door with a green Post-it attached, "I ended up truly liking the book. Thanks for letting me borrow it. Lily."

I prayed that he was still in bed, sleeping in; there are too many windows for him to easily see me. Without looking back, I quickly and carefully walked away, making sure not to crunch any leaves with my footsteps. As soon as I was far enough away from his house, I ran the rest of the way to the beach, far from Carter.

It could be argued that if I really wanted to return the book without the fear of running into Carter, I could have easily sent it to him in the mail. I suppose, deep down, there was a hint of hope and a dash of desire.

I knew that seeing his car in his driveway today was an indication of a long day ahead. No doubt, as soon as Carter found the book, something would be brewing.

I laid my towel on the sand, a quarter of a mile away from Carter's house, far enough away not to run into him, but also close enough for a chance sighting.

I settled into beach mode, ready to enjoy the warm breeze and ocean spray. Minutes later, I received a text from him. Sooner than I thought.

Carter: Where are you?
Really? Clearly, I'm at the beach. What was the point of that question?
Me: On the beach.
Carter: My beach?
Your beach? Who made it your beach? I can come here if I want to.
Me: Yes

Pointless. This man drives me nuts. Why did he bother to text me if he wasn't going to come find me? He clearly knew I was at the beach.

Those two simple texts threw me off. I no longer had the capability to immerse myself at the beach and enjoy it. The ominous gray clouds were forming.

Hours went by with no word from Carter. I thought I'd try to calm my nerves by going for a walk to people watch.

It worked. I smirked as I heard women converse about their spouses and dates gone wrong while men heatedly talked about sports, all entertaining yet inconsequential conversations.

With all the conversations and group dynamics I observed, one particular guy in gray board shorts caught my eye. That's when I found out that I had an entire encyclopedia in my memory bank for gray board shorts. There were too many thoughts being thrown out at me all because of gray board shorts.

> Gray board shorts, I think Carter has gray board shorts, but so do many other guys, but those look like the gray board shorts Carter has. Maybe that's Carter—no, it can't be Carter, he couldn't have lost that much weight since I last saw him two weeks ago. He is playing sports on the beach, which he loves to do, and there's a fit girl next to him. It must be Carter since he likes fit and skinny girls... oh, he's turning around. Maybe I shouldn't stare so intently, but I want to know if it's him or not, it's definitely him. I can recognize that gut anywhere—oh no, he saw me. I

hope he didn't see me see him. Maybe it's not him, maybe I'm just imagining it's him to create more drama. What a funny story this would be to tell. I wonder how I can make it better so that I get a laugh out of someone. He's standing with his hands on his hips staring at me walking by. Any guy could be standing with his hands on his hips looking in my direction. I need to look casual, let me run my fingers through my hair and toss it. What an idiot I am. My hair is up in a ponytail, and it's ridiculously windy. I should have waved, he should have waved, why didn't he walk over to me and say hi? I shouldn't turn around to see what he's doing now, but I want to. We were only fifty feet apart, gray board shorts.

The plethora of incoherent thoughts that manifested themselves in a matter of seconds was an affirmation of my insanity. Thank goodness I still had moments when the filter between my brain and my mouth worked. I continued my walk because that's what I originally set out to do before I was so rudely interrupted by my thoughts.

On my way back, of course I looked for Carter and the blonde girl, saw them gathering their belongings, and heading back up to his house. For a brief moment, I was hopeful that it wasn't Carter and his new girl so I watched them like a hawk, praying that they would walk right past his house.

No such luck. They walked into his place. Who was I kidding? I'm so drawn to Carter, I can spot him anywhere.

I vowed not to cry as I squinted my eyes, and tried desperately to keep tears from rolling down my face. That was enough. I was ready to go home. My heart couldn't sink any lower.

I had to decompress. I was ready for the trek home, alone with my nonsensical thoughts. I threw my towel in my trunk and stepped into my car, right foot in, left foot out, half sitting, half standing. At that exact moment, my cell phone rang.

Perplexed, I stared at my phone. My heart told me it was Carter, my mind told me otherwise – it wasn't his special ringtone. My eyes showed me the truth.

Why on earth is he calling me? Alex Sartri was the name scrolling across my cell phone screen. Carter's cousin, Alex, the one I met in Greece was on the other end of that line. *When is the last time I talked to him?*

I found it rather odd that he called me on this particular day when everything was coincidentally happening. Then again, I guess that made it a perfect day for a phone call from Alex Sartri.

"Hey, Lily! It's been awhile. Carter called me and told me you were in Manhattan Beach." "Hi, Alex. It has been awhile. Yes, I'm here but I'm leaving soon."

"No, don't leave yet. I'm actually going to be there soon. Wait for me so we can hang out," he convincingly said. "Okay, I'll see you soon," I feigned excitement.

Alex and I are great friends but he lived two hours away. He was never in this part of town. But, it wouldn't make any sense if it were any other way on this backwards day. So I made my way back to the beach to wait for Alex, wondering what could possibly be in store for me next.

Years ago, Alex opted out of knowing any details about my relationship with Carter, and therefore had no clue that we were in an awkward place right now. Part of me hoped that Alex would bring Carter along with him to the beach.

I spotted Alex walking toward me, solo. Bummer. No Carter. The first thing out of his mouth, "You came all the way to Manhattan Beach to return a book to Carter?" he asked in amusement. "You could have just sent it." I mentally kicked myself for not choosing that option. Today would have been much less of a hassle. If only.

"No," I defensively said. "Oh, that's what he said on the phone," Alex casually mentioned. *Carter, you are so manipulative! Everything does not revolve around you.*

Why Carter told him I was there didn't make sense to me either. What does it matter that I'm here? I'm essentially not really there since I didn't even give him the time of day.

It was getting late and Alex and I were getting hungry. We both had mounds of beach gear and didn't feel like walking up the hill to either of our cars to drop it off before getting a bite to eat. How convenient that Alex had Carter's house key.

Carter's car was gone. He wasn't home. I suppose I should have been thankful for that evasion of confrontation.

Alex turned the key to Carter's front door ever so slowly. I couldn't wait to get inside. Even though I knew Carter wasn't home, the excitement of being back in his house, anything Carter, was pumping my adrenaline. We dropped off our belongings near the front door while I quickly scanned the house, looking for nothing in particular except a memory to hold on to.

The situation struck me as very strange: the "ex" in the empty guy's house with his cousin who is completely clueless. *Does this count as stalking? I hope not. I didn't do this on purpose.*

Thinking that dinner was going to be the end of my evening was a mistake. After dinner, Alex got a phone call from his friend, Pete. Alex was so delighted that Pete and I would finally meet, his best guy friend and his best girl friend.

Why? Why does Alex, the wrong one, love my company so much when the "other one," the one I want, is so secretive about me?

The three of us went back to the beach to throw a football around as the sun was setting. The sky with its orange and red hues illuminating the pier was too gorgeous not to photograph. Alex and Pete's shadows looked impressive in the pictures as well.

The day was finally coming to a close. Alex and I parted ways with Pete and headed back to Carter's place. The plan was to pick up our belongings and head home.

Nothing went as planned today, so why should it start now? The day wouldn't be complete without even more awkwardness. Alex and I had so much to talk about, it really had been awhile since we'd seen each other. We ended up spending another hour at Carter's place, without Carter there. All the while I was hoping and fearing Carter would come home.

Being in Carter's house was overwhelming. The minute we walked in, his scent rushed to greet me at the door as if someone had a fan turned on, wafting his essence in my direction. Everything about that man drives me crazy.

I so badly wanted to go into Carter's bedroom but thought otherwise as long as Alex was there. *Didn't he have to go to the bathroom?* The instant Alex got up to use the bathroom, I rushed to Carter's room. I only had a few precious minutes before I had to sit back down and position myself exactly the way I was.

Opening the door to his bedroom was like winning the jackpot at a casino in Las Vegas. The satisfaction of basking in Carter's overpowering scent instantly plastered a silly grin on my face. *I love it!*

I suddenly had the urge to find out what he did with the book I returned to him that morning. I listened for a flushed toilet or running water. Nope. That bought me another minute.

I wanted to know if Carter threw the book on his desk, on the floor, or on the bed, not knowing what that would prove once I found it. I truly wasn't trying to be a snoop, just curious is all.

I quickly spotted it on his nightstand, with the Post-it still on it. My heart did a little flutter. Being a silly girl, I figured he didn't take my Post-it off because he wanted some kind of reminder of me. I just stared at it, overjoyed.

I heard the water turn off in the bathroom. How could I have missed the flush of the toilet? I quickly scanned Carter's bedroom one last time, tried to commit it to memory, took in one more breath of his scent, and quietly closed his door, positioning myself back on the couch, desperately trying to wipe the grin off my face.

Alex's oblivion couldn't have been more welcome. Enough was enough. It was time to go home on a good note. What an exhausting day.

I got home around ten thirty and went straight to bed, only to be woken up by a text from Carter at one in the morning. I'm still involved in drama, even while I sleep! "Thanks for the call," he texted with sarcasm. I couldn't hear his voice but I knew it was sarcasm. *You don't deserve a response. Sorry Carter.* As much as I was irritated, my delight trumped any negative feelings I had.

What did today mean? I could sit and analyze my entire day for the fiftieth time, thinking about all the what-if's, but all in all, it truly was a perfectly ridiculous day.

I couldn't contain my excitement. Despite my exhaustion, I was wide awake. *Why not? Let me analyze today one more time.*

I always like to think that my gut feeling is right, that my womanly intuition is purposeful. Scrutinizing every detail one more time, I laid in bed giving myself a Cliff Notes rundown of the day's events.

Carter texted me to make some sort of connection with me because he wanted to see me. But, for some reason he made zero effort. When I saw him on the beach with a girl, most likely "the girl" I got dumped for, I figured he was spending the day with her all along. He was guilt-tripping me into thinking that I had a duty to see him when I was in his neck of the woods. Even if I did try to see him, he probably would have told me he was busy. Typical Assface behavior—possessive like the world owes him something because he's good-looking.

Thursday, June 24, 2010

Thank goodness I left for San Francisco today. This road trip with two great friends was exactly what I needed to get my mind off the absurd drama from the day before.

The day started off on the right foot—great weather, great people, great fun. We got to our hotel late in the afternoon, and I decided to check my e-mail. As soon as I signed on, that boy instant messaged me on Gchat. *Leave me alone! You can't have me and that stupid convenient girl, whom you don't even really like!*

> Carter: so u saw my car at my house and didn't want to say hi?
> Me: didn't want to bother you
> Carter: hmm
> Me: you knew I was there and didn't call me
> Carter: um, cuz I figured that u didn't want to talk to me or see me if ur the one who saw my car there.
> Me: you knew I was there and didn't bother calling me
> Carter: cuz I figured u didn't want me to. YOU knew I was there first and u didn't bother to call or even notify me. clearly u would have at least texted me saying u were out there unless u didn't want me to know u were
> Me: ok...I'm not sure I'm ready to see you anytime soon
> Carter: so then why'd u come to my beach
> Me: because I like your beach and how was I supposed to know you would be home in the middle of the week... you're supposed to be at work
> Carter: so then u stayed at my beach and just hoped u wouldn't see me?
> Me: ok so I saw you...so what? you saw me too. I don't want to see you anymore.
> Carter: wow

What is this convict's logic, trying to make me feel bad? He did me wrong, yet it's my fault that our relationship is at a standstill.

How many times did he say he didn't think I wanted to see him and he didn't want to bother me? You'd think he said it enough times to believe it, but apparently not. When I *actually* blatantly told him that I don't want to see him, he went into shock. After showing my sister this conversation, she said, "I'm not sure if he's hurt or butt hurt."

"Ha, what's the difference?" I asked.

"Huuuge difference," my sister emphasized. "If he's hurt, then he understands that he has a part in your pain, but if he's butt hurt, then he just feels sorry for himself and thinks that you are out of line for not wanting to see him."

My little big sister. I sometimes forget that I'm older than her.

Given my past experiences with him, I would say he thinks the latter. I don't think he'll ever grow up. Yet, I will still patiently and foolishly wait around for the day he *might* mature.

Friday, June 25, 2010

Carter-free day? Ha! I don't even know what it's like to not think about Carter at least thirteen times a day. Although I may not see him as often as I'd like, he's still my first and last thought every morning and every night. I haven't had a peaceful day in my brain for the last ten years. It's like having a nasty twitch; you just adapt.

The day I don't think about him at all will be a historic day of earth-shattering celebrations. I might even invite him to the party. *Wait, I can't do that.* That would be counterproductive.

Oh yeah, by the way, I found out today that the offer I put on a townhouse, my very first home, was accepted. That is huge news, but it took a backseat to Carter, just like everything else in my life. Maybe this is the project I was looking for to keep my mind off him.

Saturday, June 26, 2010

Weddings have always been a place of major dancing and festivity for me. Today's wedding didn't quite have that effect on me.

Most everyone came with a significant other, and those who didn't, ended up too drunk from drowning themselves in their sorrow. What's a girl to do?

Instead of sifting through the few sorrowful drunks to find dance partners or join them in their drunken misery, I thought about how Carter and I should be getting married.

Looking around and seeing most people as half of a pair didn't put me in the best mood. I could have done without this wedding. *Sorry friends. Please don't take offense to that comment.*

My mind was on Carter, and Carter was on my mind. Any way you look at it, Carter was there as I was sitting in the hotel room after the wedding, mindlessly surfing the Internet. The phone rang, I picked it up, heard a girl talking, but my mind heard Carter talking.

"Hey, it's Carter," the voice on the other end of the phone said. I couldn't quite figure out what was happening. *It's a female voice, but it's Carter?* Silence on my end.

"Hello, Lily, are you there?" the voice questioned. Finally, after hearing her voice again, my mind registered who was on the other end of the line. My friend Carterina, goes by Carter.

All I heard was that name that made my heart skip a beat and my stomach do somersaults. It took me way too long to realize that *my* Carter wasn't calling. My jumbled thoughts couldn't even sort out the fact that Carter is not a girl.

Even the sound of his name has a resounding effect on me. I couldn't help but laugh at my ridiculousness.

Sunday, June 27, 2010

It was a long drive home from San Francisco to Los Angeles. As usual, there was a whirlwind of Carter thoughts in my brain, so I took a nap. Thankfully, I had no dreams.

Even though they obviously aren't real, dreams make me so emotional, even more so than my daily fleeting thoughts. My mind took the time to emerge from its deep dark cave to show me what my subconscious was thinking. I should respect that. I feel so vulnerable when I can recall a dream.

Late that night, when I got home, I posted my pictures of the sunset, Alex, and Pete, from my ridiculous Wednesday in Manhattan Beach, on Facebook.

Monday, June 28, 2010

Back to another week of work. I was demoralized, so much so that one of my coworkers instantly noticed the flatness of my step and attributed it to Assface striking again. Guess I'm not good at separating my personal life from work.

I filled in my coworker, Yvonne, about my Carter saga despite knowing the scolding I would get. Somehow, I didn't care. I just liked talking about him and hearing the sound of his name roll off my tongue.

If I'm ever going to get a text from Stupid Boy, I can almost guarantee it will be right around midnight. What I can't guarantee, however, is when I will be getting a text. So, to my surprise, particularly since I told him I didn't want to talk to him a few days earlier, he texted me.

> Carter: Again u were at my beach and didn't text hello?
> And hung out with my cousin? Grr

Of course, this caused a major commotion, even though I was already in bed sleeping. By the way, did I mention that he has his own ring tone and text message sound? I immediately know if that boy is communicating with me.

I've been conditioned to salivate at the sound of his text message notification or ring tone. This isn't really strange, though, considering that when instant messaging grew popular, he also had his own alert, the sound of a cow mooing. To this day, any slight cow noise and my heart starts beating like crazy while I smile uncontrollably.

The text didn't make sense to me. I didn't go back to "his" beach. What was he talking about? I woke my sister up from her deep sleep just to help me analyze Carter's 17 word text. There was no way I was going to wait until morning to talk to her.

Disoriented, she finally gathered her thoughts an eternity later while I impatiently waited, as if she owed me her two cents.

"He's drunk," was all she could come up with. Irritated with that answer, I snapped, "Just go back to bed." I didn't want to equate my worth to a drunk text from Carter.

I looked for my dad in search of a better explanation. Being a workaholic, he was still awake past midnight. "Dad!" I exclaimed. "What is Carter doing?" I asked exasperated.

"Don't respond, just wait," he calmly explained. "This guy likes you, probably more than that girl he's with, but he doesn't know what to do with you. Trust me, I know guys. He'll come back to you when he's done with that girl."

He told me exactly what I wanted to hear. With every word my dad spoke, my grin spread a little wider. I love it when people tell me what I want to hear about Carter Swinton.

Perfect! Thanks, dad. Now I can go back to bed and sleep restfully.

Tuesday, June 29, 2010

I got it! I understood what he meant by that text. I must have had a dream that revealed the answer to me in my subconscious because I thought I had a dreamless night.

He must have seen my Facebook pictures from Manhattan Beach, the ones I posted on Sunday, four days after the actual event. So many things about this situation made me smile, literally from ear to ear. For sure my face isn't big enough for the size of my smile.

In order for him to see the pictures, he must have looked at my Facebook. Score! He wanted to see what's up in my life. Because I posted the pictures days later, he must have assumed I drove down to Manhattan Beach a second time without acknowledging him. Score again! He got jealous that I spent time with his cousin. And...he growled at me. Who growls? He so misses me.

Trying to get over someone who's not letting you let go is extremely difficult. He's giving me hope. There's no way I can close the chapter on this dude. He's not letting the saga end.

My mommy and I decided to spend some time together and watched *Toy Story 3*. It should have been a nice, relaxing night out with no interruptions from Carter. But, he just won't leave me alone. There is always some sort of connection to that man, who is still really a boy. (Maybe I just manage to find a connection so that I don't have to let go of him). One of the voices of the characters is performed by Carter's uncle. Even the movie reminded me of Carter.

Wednesday, June 30, 2010

I miss his smile. I miss the way he looks at me with those soft ocean-blue eyes. I miss the way his eyes speak thousands of words without his lips moving. I miss feeling his eyes on me when I look away. I miss his tender touch. I miss how he makes my dopamine levels go all silly. I miss him so much I read past online conversations with him when we were on good terms. I miss him good.

Thursday, July 1, 2010

The first day of July. It was time to rebuild my life. My life was falling apart because it needed to. It needed to because it wasn't built the right way in the first place.

I know that in comparison to the majority of the population, my life is not a mess. But, loving a boy who doesn't love me back is the worst thing that could happen to me. That was my biggest dream as a child; to live happily ever after with my prince.

Thinking that I found my prince and having him toss me to the wayside is more than enough to qualify my life as fallen apart. Broken heart equals broken life.

Carter and I don't have a healthy relationship. Check. We started on the wrong foot to begin with. Check. Carter and I need to be rebuilt with a better foundation. I know we can start fresh and get through this together.

I felt very philosophical and poetic today as I recalled a verse from Yvette Samaan's poem, *I Can Cry Later.*

> "I can cry later
> Now it's time to live,
> I'll be sad later
> Now it's time to give."

This is the first day of July! It was time to rebuild my life. If I kept telling myself, then it would become a reality. This is going to be the start of something good.

Boys always come up in conversation with teen girls. It's no surprise that in class today, two girls started boy bashing and included me in the conversation. So of course, I had to tell them about Carter Swinton. The world would be at a loss if I didn't tell everyone I know about that fool.

I love that high school girls are very dramatic. They "ahh" and "ohh" in all the right places. They made me feel like I was a first class storyteller. Teenagers are the best audience for storytelling. They are captivated by anything that is not school related and keeps them from doing work.

Now my high-schoolers know about Carter. I swear I think *every* person I've ever come across, even for a brief moment, could speak at my wedding and attest to my obsession with the guy. (I still think it's love).

During my lunch break, I ran an errand and drove by Morado Road. Sadly, I remembered where this whole breakup shenanigan first took place. However, I drove by Morado Road five cities over. It was a completely different road with no correlation whatsoever to the other one.

There is no way anyone can convince me that there aren't signs that Carter and I are destined to be together. How can anyone deny the hard facts? He's all around me.

After work, I tutor. Because I go to the students' homes, I have become part of their lives, and they have become a part of mine. I am always treated as one of the family, another daughter. It's no surprise that they ask me about my love life.

On this particular day, the mother asked me if "that boy" had tried contacting me since we broke up. She vaguely knew the story of Carter and me, so I had to choose wisely. If I said "no," that would be the end of the conversation, but if I said "yes," I would give myself an opportunity to talk about Carter.

Knowing that I'd probably spend an extra half an hour, possibly making me late for my next appointment, I went with a meek "yes."

How is it that Carter invades every crevice of my brain? How is it that I'm bursting at the seams with Carter? How is it that everyone sees him as poison, yet I see him as honey? My mom would often, sadly say, "You're drowning in your own love, it's dysfunctional. You're a classic case of madly in love."

"Honey, can you come here please?" she immediately hollered to her husband across the house. I couldn't believe she interrupted his work to have him listen to my situation. It made me feel like my story was worthy of being told multiple times.

"Honey, can you help us figure out what's wrong with this boy, from a man's point of view?" "Lily, tell him your story, so he can analyze his actions," she prompted.

I told the story *again*. The *entire* story. (This must be my twenty-third time telling it, and it never gets old). I somehow always find new people to tell.

We discovered that this family used to live exactly one block away from where Carter lives now, on the same street. They were only a stone's throw away. I know they don't live there now, but still, it's too crazy a coincidence. It's a sign! Carter is destined to be with me. It's clearly in the stars.

As the half hour mark passed, I gave up trying to end the discussion. I can go hours talking about Carter and this family was willing to listen.

I never cease to be amazed with what new information comes up about Assface. As we were finally wrapping up the gossip, the mother mentioned her frequent trips to Manhattan Beach. Clearly enjoying being an informant, she mentioned that last time she went, she saw a bunch of heavily perfumed girls with too much makeup walk into a condo near Carter's place. Ha! My own personal private detective! She's going to be a terrific spy.

Friday, July 2, 2010

I texted my ex-boyfriend, Rico. We broke up recently at the beginning of February this year. It had been about five months since we'd spoken.

After he proposed to me and I responded with, "I don't know," we were done. He countered with, "We've invested too much time into each other, and if you don't know by now, you'll never know." So that was it. We called it quits after almost three years.

I missed Rico, but not nearly as much as I missed Carter Swinton.

Rico texted me back. Turns out he missed me too. We made plans to go to the beach together tomorrow. *Please, please, please, don't let me be acting on a rebound with him. I've already hurt him so much.*

Saturday, July 3, 2010

At the beach, Rico and I picked up right where we left off. There wasn't a moment of silence. We were both beaming. It was so natural to spend time with him. It truly made me wonder why we didn't work. I considered him my best friend. He was so supportive and such a good listener. He's got the kindest soul despite his tough exterior.

As if reading my mind, Rico veered the conversation into dangerous territory; why we broke up. When I thought we had beaten the horse to death, Rico brought up other points. *I knew this was a bad idea. He's still not over me.*

Then, he dropped the bomb. "Over the past few months, I've been dating a girl pretty seriously," Rico reluctantly mentioned. I sarcastically thought, "so serious that you're willing to spend all day with your ex and discuss reasons why we should still be together."

There it was again. It seemed to pop up more often these days. That smug look when I knew the ball was in my court, that I had the power.

Sadly, it didn't make a difference whether I held the reins or not. Rico should have been out of my life. I wasn't going back to him. He wasn't right for me, despite my brief thoughts otherwise this morning.

Bless his heart. He tried so hard to make me jealous by pausing before continuing but I saw right through him. His eyes were the windows to his soul. I knew she wasn't a keeper.

Confirming my thoughts, Rico said, "It didn't work. She didn't pass the Lily test." Silence from both of us. Silence from him out of embarrassment and silence from me out of sympathy. *Isn't this exactly what I despised about Assface? The mixed messages.*

Those few seconds seemed an eternity as we just stared into each other's eyes, trying to speak volumes without uttering any words. Shattering the silence, Rico whispered, "I compare everyone to you." All of a sudden, there was a bittersweet taste in my mouth.

On the one hand, it was the best compliment a girl could get. But on the other hand, it was a slap in the face. He still loved me and was hopeful that we would get back together someday.

Is this how pathetic I've become? The tables were turned, and I was on the other end. Essentially, I was Carter, selfish Assface who wants to keep me in his life because he knows I love him, and Rico was me, hopeless romantic who believes that love will find a way.

I cared very deeply for Rico, but I truly didn't think we were compatible. Being selfish, I wanted to incorporate him in my life even if that meant hurting him by not being with him.

The right thing to do would be to part ways, but I couldn't bear to lose someone I cared for and whom I knew would go to the ends of the earth for me.

Maybe one day Rico will be the right person for me. This must be how Carter thinks about me. I'm the backup girl he likes having around because I give him attention. But, he doesn't really want to commit because he doesn't think we are compatible.

What a beautiful mess. Rico is in love with me, I'm in love with Carter, and Carter is not in love with me. (In my opinion, I think he's just confused). What a twisted chain of love.

The way Rico had been looking at me all day would have made any girl melt, but I stayed strong. I was already too bruised to get into any type of pseudo relationship.

Humans have this funny way of torturing each other. Despite all the love in his heart for me, Rico asked me about Carter, if things had progressed.

I kept it simple, "Carter and I didn't work." Just as Rico's eyes were the windows to his soul, my eyes were even bigger sparkling windows, clearly displaying what was inside.

He immediately knew that I still cared very deeply for that stupid man who's consumed my life. Instantly his face fell, and it broke my heart to see him hurt. I can't even pretend not to like Carter.

Sunday, July 4, 2010

Happy Fourth of July to me, wallowing in my pity. Seeing Rico yesterday was a terrible mistake. I've opened his wound and rubbed salt in it and what is this feeling? *I miss Rico?!* I have no idea what I'm doing. I can't stop thinking about Carter, and now I've thrown Rico back into the mix just for kicks.

Am I an attention whore? If I can't have attention from one guy, will I search for someone who will give me attention? I'm creating unnecessary drama, as usual. I just can't sit still. Now that I'm feeling miserable, I don't feel like wanting to be strong today.

I've been taking many steps forward on my road to recovery. However, today I took a step backward. I looked at Carter's Facebook, which I miraculously managed to avoid for the last month. I found a few pictures of him and his new girlfriend. The strangest thing happened; I started laughing.

She was *nothing* close to who he usually dates. *Hmm, that's interesting.* She's blonde (he's always liked brunettes) and has very large breasts, possibly fake (he doesn't even like big boobs). She's a professional cheerleader for beach volleyball.

I knew better than to stoop down to this level, but I took a minute to stereotype and judge her right at that moment. This was my take on her. She's a blonde dancer with a good body. To me that means she has an open schedule, is available to have sex and party anytime, and is uneducated, which basically translates to a "just for now" girl.

Carter!! What are you thinking? This is the girl he left me for. The caliber of the woman he chose after me was at least seventy-five notches below me. That's an insult to me, Carter Swinton.

Facebook is the demise of my generation. I can snoop and stalk all I want without anyone knowing, and the only side effect is depression and insanity. This man—excuse me, this boy, excuse me, this Assface—has no idea what he wants. He just wants to play around and sow his wild oats. Fine!

But don't come crying to me when this relationship fails due to lack of intelligent conversations. When the sex gets old and boring, nothing will be left. Have fun trying to get me back, jerk. The sad reality is I'll probably still be waiting and take him back in a second.

Monday, July 5, 2010

Why are dreams so elusive, yet so influential in my life? I am so confused. I am a classic example of a head case or a hot mess, or maybe both.

You'd think that since I just spent the day with Rico, I'd dream about him instead of the "other one." It's been established that my life doesn't follow any routine rhythm. What I expect and what actually happen seem to be polar opposites.

In my dream, I was at Manhattan Beach, walking around by myself, when all of a sudden, I had an immediate urge, just like a child, to go to the bathroom.

There were no bathrooms in sight, but Carter's place was right around the corner. Although I didn't want to see him, I walked to his house half hoping he'd be home but also half hoping he wouldn't be home. I'm always so conflicted about seeing him, even apparent in my dreams.

His front door was wide open and his house was filled with people just hanging out. I figured that if I walked in and used the bathroom, no one would even notice.

As I walked toward the bathroom in the back of the house, the crowd of people thinned out, and I saw his girlfriend sitting on the floor doing homework. It appeared that she was still in high school. (I believe this was my way of projecting that I think she's uneducated). *Gross*, I think. *She's totally beneath you, Carter, but maybe that's why you want her—so you can be better than her.*

I quickly avoided eye contact with her but instead, out of habit, I walked into Carter's bedroom. Two steps in, I saw him with his back toward the door, and I sprinted out. I wasn't even sure why I walked in. It was those pesky conflicting thoughts about seeing him kicking in again.

The plan was to stealthily go to the bathroom and sneak back out unnoticed. He didn't see me. What an awkward situation that would have been, me, "the ex," in his room while his girlfriend was in the other room, studying.

I rushed to the bathroom, closed the door, leaned with my back against it, and slid down. *You're wearing yourself out, Lily. Just get out of there.* Just as I turned the water off to dry my hands, I saw the door handle rattle. I quickly glanced at the lock, thankful that I remembered to push it in despite my rush.

Someone else needed to use the bathroom. No problem as long as it wasn't Carter. I hoped and prayed that it was one of the other million guests instead. But because my life was that ironic, I already knew that anyone other than Carter on the other side of that bathroom door was wishful thinking.

I opened the door and was face to face with Carter, standing there with a look of shock on his face. "What are you doing here?" he imploringly asked. "You can't be here."

"I was using the bathroom and was on my way out," I said as calmly as I could.

No more words were spoken. We briefly gazed at each other a little too long; there was clearly tension there. I unwillingly broke our gaze, pushed past him, and silently walked out.

As I walked out, that jerk slapped my ass, with his girlfriend in the other room. Outwardly, I had to pretend to be appalled by his behavior because it was supposed to be inappropriate. But inwardly, I was cheering; I loved it. It made me feel like I had the upper hand. That girl had nothing on me.

I looked him straight in the eye, articulated, "You can't be doing that," and walked out.

That was the most promising dream I've had in a long time. There was hope.

Rico once told me that passion inspires and obsession consumes. As much as I'd like to ignore the hard facts, it's impossible to deny that at this point, Carter doesn't inspire me; he consumes me.

Tuesday, July 6, 2010

The days after a holiday are always incredibly difficult at work. Nonetheless, I was in good spirits today.

Last night, my best friend, Anna, came over, and we had a blast laughing like little girls. Life was good. It got even better today with a random instant message from Carter. "Hope you had a nice Fourth," he wrote.

Of course, an unwilling smile snuck up on my face. He was fueling my fire and giving me more ammunition to prove that he still wanted me.

I did my best to ignore the message, and against my will, I didn't respond. Inside I was kicking and screaming. I think I made the right decision, but not before calling my dad immediately after he messaged me to get some advice.

I went about my day, checked my Facebook and noticed that my relationship status had "changed" to Single. The catch, however, was that I had been single on Facebook for over a year, so I wasn't really sure what happened there. Must have been a glitch in Facebook. Technology works against us sometimes.

I received so many wall posts and messages asking if I was okay and if it was Assface/Carter/Swinton/jerk/USC/"the face"/ church camp guy who broke my heart. (He has many names, these are just a few). Again, I didn't do anything to bring this kind of attention upon myself, yet he was being thrown into my life without fair warning at the most obscure times.

It also reminded me that most of my 1,600 plus friends on Facebook were aware of my Carter enigma and that almost no one knew that I had been with Rico for almost three years. With that realization came another; I was so glad Rico didn't have a Facebook to witness the wall posts. They were coming in too fast for me to delete them immediately. He would have died and I surely would have been accused of Facebook murder.

I unglued myself from the computer to go tutor. The family who used to live in Manhattan Beach told me they went yesterday and were looking all over for Carter. They looked for his car and walked by his place many times, to no avail. This was truly ridiculous, and I loved it. It gave me a good laugh, and God knows I needed it.

Who knows why they were so interested in finding out about Carter but it gave me comfort knowing that he would be under the microscope by someone other than me.

Wednesday, July 7, 2010

Ehh! Blah! Nothing special. Finally an uneventful day in terms of Carter. It didn't mean he wasn't on my mind. It just meant he wasn't brought up in conversation with anyone.

Thursday, July 8, 2010

I almost got through the day without mentioning him, but then dinner happened. As soon as I thought I had no one else to tell my Carter story to, someone I hadn't spoken to for a while popped into my life.

Since everyone knew about Swinton, everyone always asked to be updated about our status. In reality, I almost never bring him up. I did an excellent job carving the way for people to ask about him by planting the seeds of my obsession stories early on.

My friend Tracy was visiting from New York and called to schedule a last minute dinner with me. She asked about Assface. I almost cried while updating her on my sad love story. He *still* got to me.

After dinner, I received a phone call from Eric. You know it, I got to tell my story one more time today to someone whose opinion mattered the most—his cousin and my best friend, Eric.

His cousin is my best friend—that's a clear indicator that our lives should be intertwined. Shouldn't this be, "I already have family approval?" since I am so close with so many of his cousins.

Literally, I am great friends with three of his male cousins. At one point or another, each of the other three were interested in me, and I've interlaced fingers and held hands with all four of them. I could be such a hand whore sometimes.

This time, as I recapped my story yet *again*, I was more passionate about it, more emotional. Maybe it was because Eric was the only person I've told who knows Carter.

As sad as that sounds, not a single one of my friends had met Carter. All everyone knew of him were the nicknames I gave him and the stories I've told. Since I really only told the bad stories, no one liked him and was very subjective and biased when giving advice.

But Eric is his cousin who grew up with him and knows both of us very well. He was there from the very beginning when Carter and I met.

I held nothing back telling Eric, although I was hesitant at first to divulge any details to his cousin. I didn't want to involve him in any family drama—or worse yet, have him take sides.

Alex, Eric's brother, opted out of hearing any stories about Carter and me years ago because, as he put it, "Carter is my cousin, and he can do no wrong, and I really just don't want to know. He's my cousin, and you're a good friend. It would be awkward."

Fair enough. Jacob, one of the other cousins, was completely out of the loop with my situation, as he should be. He had tried to date me on numerous occasions, and truly liked me. He would have been devastated if he found out that Carter and I had major chemistry.

Eric, on the other hand, let me spill it all out; and for the first time, I heard unskewed feedback. Eric was such a great friend. He let me talk about Carter for hours. I even told him about Rico and the "Lily test."

To my surprise, he mentioned that he had his own "Lily test." He said, "If every guy had a 'Lily test' no guy would be dating any girl. You're just that great, Lily."

Everyone thinks I'm great. Just not Carter Swinton. My story was so heartfelt that Eric teared up. I should make a movie about this, I think. My sob story is a tearjerker, which is pretty much the only criterion for a chick flick. This is brilliant.

Eric basically told me that I'm Carter's backup girl, the best friend, the confidante, the girl he can always count on, the girl he loves and cares very deeply for but doesn't know what to do with just quite yet. He went on to say that his current dancer/cheerleader girlfriend is just for fun and that he's just showing off to the world that he can get a chick like that.

"He'll never marry her," he said with conviction. "But you two have history, and he will come back to you. You two have a cycle. At least he's figuring things out. It's a step toward the right direction. He's growing up, but you need to let him have his fun."

Fine!

Eric clearly saw Carter's actions as progress. I'm not sure what exactly I missed, but I saw his action of "dumping" me as idiotic. Maybe in a few years, I will look back on this situation and, in retrospect, realize that it was a monumentally great moment when he decided to kick me to the curb for a dumb blonde. (She may not be dumb, but in my mind, she is, and it makes me feel better to say so).

"By the way," he said, "did you know that when Carter first met you all he could talk about was how perfect you would be for me? He was adamantly trying to set us up."

What?!

Interesting. Carter was majorly flirting with me when he first met me. He was so ridiculously complex yet simple at the same time. He was like a little boy with a crush on a girl, trying to pass her off to the next guy in hopes that he'd still be in contact with her if he played matchmaker.

Now that I thought about it, it made perfect sense. He had such low self-esteem. He must have thought that I would never go for him, so instead of losing me from his life, he found an opportunity to include me in his life by giving me to his cousin.

How ironic. This story just gets more and more bizarre. I'm no longer shocked by any twists and loops in our roller-coaster of a story. Our saga is not meant to be bland.

Friday, July 9, 2010

I noticed that he didn't come online as much, he never had a status message anymore, and he never had a green dot next to his name. (It was always red or orange, meaning that he was always busy).

I wonder if that had *anything* to do with me. It made me feel like his away messages were for me to read and comment on, almost like an icebreaker or conversation starter.

The thought crossed my mind, though, of how long I would journal for. When would I be at a point in my life where Carter didn't affect me, or at least only minimally?

This diary stuff is therapeutic, but I can't do it forever. I want there to be an ending to this story, preferably a happy ending where Carter and I get married.

Someone else found me today and asked about Carter. I got to tell the story again to my friend Rachel, who lives in England. It's been a month, and he's just about invaded every single day.

Saturday, July 10, 2010

I was a little distracted today, to say the least. A childhood friend on Facebook chatted me up last night and asked to go out on a date. All day today, I thought about how ironic it was that Reed and I used to be neighbors, three houses down, but never really hung out, and now he was asking me out. I always had a little crush on him. Life is funny.

The one thing in life that keeps my thoughts at bay instead of racing around is fitness. I *love* anything that has to do with fitness. I am *that* passionate about it that it will override my self-diagnosed paralysis of the heart-broken.

The calmness and focus that fitness brings to my mind is nothing less of a miracle. I was in heaven today because Carter didn't enter my mind since I was so preoccupied with being enlightened about group fitness classes during a fitness seminar.

During class, we were paired up with someone in order to critique our teaching style. Of course, I was paired up with a girl who had some faint connection to Carter.

We chatted a bit, as it turns out, she was an active member of the church where Carter grew up. I had to stop myself from asking if she knew him.

Really?!

Even on the day when I'm supposed to have no distractions I was bombarded with Carter. There was no avoiding him. I have never had a more difficult time trying to avoid someone I don't even see very often.

Sunday, July 11, 2010

I might be outgrowing the diarying soon. (I like that word better than *journaling* even though it sounds like I have bathroom issues).

Earlier, I wanted to stop tracking my progress because I thought it was taking over my life. Now I don't want to stop. It's as if this is my last connection to him. If I stop, I may never have any more chances to reminisce about him. I'm scared to live a life without Carter's invasive presence somewhere in my mind. It's all I've known for the better part of my life. It's like losing a pet no matter how much trouble they were.

I just recently put down my dog, Fluffy, after fifteen wonderful years. I got her when I was in eighth grade, so she's been a huge part of my life.

Despite the fact that she had *many* potty accidents over the years, particularly in her old age, and stank up the house, I never wanted her out of my life. Even though it was better for her to go to doggy heaven, I still get nostalgic and truly miss her.

This is how I feel about Carter. He's a burden to me, yet I don't want him out of my life. I still have Fluffy's clothes and collar and can't bear to part with them—similar to how I can't part with my leopard box full of Carter memorabilia. Neither way gives me comfort: life with or without Carter.

I take it back. No amount of distractions, fitness or no fitness, can be enough to have Carter seep out of my life.

I rented a movie my friend recommended, not knowing much about it. Of course, the main character's name had to be Carter. I just can't get away from him!

Everything is a constant reminder of him. Let me be positive; as long as that was the only Carter association I made, then today was a pretty mild day in terms of Carter action.

But, my life seemed to be made for drama, and there was no such thing as simple for me. At around 10:30 p.m., my cell phone rang and as if on cue, my heart turned in vain hope for Carter.

It was Alex, Carter's cousin. Disappointed, but equally excited to catch up with him, we talked for hours.

It was still inevitable that Carter came up in conversation. There was always much simultaneous heartache and happiness when he was brought up.

On the one hand, I enjoyed hearing updates about his life and what he was doing because it made me feel involved. On the other hand, I didn't like hearing about his exciting life that he shared with another girl. Not that Alex was being insensitive, but he was unaware of the dynamics between Carter and me.

I found out that Alex was going to be Carter's roommate and he was going to start working for Carter's dad. Here came the scheming crew from the dusty corners of my mind.

Alex's ever present proximity to Carter would mean a constant flow of Carter information and inclusion of activities with Carter there. I'm Alex's best girlfriend, and Alex is Carter's favorite cousin, so I was bound to run into Carter at some point. Oh, how I loved scheming.

Monday, July 12, 2010

I am such a Facebook stalker. I know everything there possibly is to know about Carter through Facebook, and what's more, I know as much about all his Facebook friends.

When I am introduced to any of his friends through Alex, I feel like we are old buddies. I truly have to be careful not to act as if I know them, which is getting to be difficult. At this point, everyone in Carter's life looks like a familiar face to me. (Thank you, Facebook).

I called T-Mobile customer service today to find out the status of my rebate. It was no surprise that the phone operator's name was Carter. I know it's a common name, but gosh darn it, I've never run into so many Carters in my life.

I noticed that I've been referring to him with his name more often rather than "Assface" or any other crude nickname I've given him in the past. I must not be as angry with him anymore.

God was giving me the strength to get through this time of my life, and boy did I need it given the extensive history and curveballs being thrown my way every day.

Tuesday, July 13, 2010

I went out to dinner with Reed, the childhood friend I reconnected with through Facebook. The date was good but not Carter good.

Wednesday, July 14, 2010

Let's see how many Carters I can be associated with in one day. I got a new student today. His name was Carter. Carter, a childhood friend decided to call and catch up today. Another friend, Carter, invited me to his birthday dinner after work. And, at 1:00 p.m., Carter Swinton instant messaged me, "Hope ur doing well," which led to a smile, which then led to butterflies and somersaults in my stomach.

Again with the non-questions. I'm not going to respond to non-questions. I don't know what his goal was if he wasn't asking me questions. That boy is a conundrum. What's worse is that all I know for sure is that I don't know why he does what he does or how to respond to it. All I have are my educated assumptions. So, why can't I let go of the unknown?

Every time I hear from him, I reflexively put on an expression of impassioned nostalgia. I've been conditioned to love him with all my heart.

Today was also the first day since the "breakup" that he put up a status message: "Yo! semite.wknd." I can almost guarantee that he messaged me today because he wanted to bring attention to the fact that he would be traveling. By messaging me, it forced me to notice his boastful status, killing two birds with one stone.

He's such a conniving showoff. He's definitely an undercover competitor with me. He wants to one-up me without really saying so or rubbing it in my face. I suppose that's sweet. Men these days.

Thursday, July 15, 2010

Today should have been special. Today would have been ten years. Today, I couldn't believe I pined over Carter since I first met him on July 15, 2000. Today, I was taking my life back.

My coworker had been going through a rough patch with her man. She gave me a piece of her mind the moment she walked into work.

> "Why is it that when it comes to love relationships, we want one particular person? If you think about it, we really just want to be happy with the perfect *person*. But we try to mold who we want into the perfect person and get upset with God for not listening to us. But, the reality is, God knows much more and sees the message loud and clear: in thirty years, the bliss and happiness you deserve won't happen in the relationship you want so badly. Why is it that we think we know more than God, who can see everything?"

She must have read something inspiring last night. It was painfully true, but I was still going to tell the universe what I wanted. There's no harm in nagging.

I liked what she said so I typed it up, laminated it, and it's going to go into my leopard box of Carter memorabilia. One day, when we get married, I'll give him that box as a wedding gift.

Oh, did I mention that already? It must be because I want it to happen so terribly badly.

Friday, July 16, 2010

Carter was on Gchat all day today. All day today, I felt like a donkey with a carrot dangling just inches from my face, barely out of reach. I saw the temptation but couldn't do anything about it.

I'm not *allowed* to instant message him even though there are so many things I want to say to him. *Why did you leave me? How was Yosemite? Do you miss me? Why do you bother contacting me?* I could go on forever with questions to ask Carter, all of which are meaningless in the grand scheme of my situation right now.

My rulebook specifically says I can't instant message Carter or contact him unless he directly asks me a question. (I make up the rules as I see fit and go along through life).

My friend Carter Movelli is right underneath Carter Swinton on my Gchat buddy list. Carter Movelli is basically Carter Swinton.

They are both named Carter, both attended USC for their undergraduate degree in business, Pepperdine for law school, and traveled the same study abroad trips that were offered through school. Most importantly, they are similar looking, gorgeous blue eyes and a head full of dirty blonde hair that curls around their ears.

Every time I attempt to instant message him, Carter Movelli, I almost hope that I'll have a slip of the mouse and accidentally message Carter Swinton instead. I mean, I do and I don't. I would be violating my rulebook if I messaged him. It's so difficult being me.

Saturday, July 17, 2010

Because Carter Movelli is so similar to Carter Swinton, going out with Movelli would almost be like going out with Swinton. If I fantasize just enough, the two are interchangeable.

As it turned out, tonight was one of those nights. I went out with a group of friends to the Magic Castle, an exclusive magic club where you must be dressed up to enter. I was with friends from different groups, and apparently, I was acting as if Carter Movelli were my boyfriend because many of my friends asked if we were together. I don't even like the guy, or do I?

I'm so confused. I think I was just *pretending* that he was Swinton because he's close enough.

Sunday, July 18, 2010

I must not have heard my text message alert. Once again, in vain hope, I watched the name scroll across my cell phone screen, as if I were waiting for my scores after competing in the Olympics. "New message Carter…" and didn't see *Movelli* until seconds later, but it was already too late.

My stomach was already flipping all over the place. I got way too excited over a dumb text that, even if it was from Stupid Boy, I wouldn't have responded because I'm not allowed to.

And I thought I was making progress. Apparently not. I may have even started back at square negative three. (I'm a math teacher. I had to make my point).

I talked to Alex on the phone today. He was at Carter's house. I had to cut the conversation short simply so I would refrain from asking about Carter or telling Alex to say "hello" to him.

Woman! Where is your self-control? Apparently, I have none when it comes to AF. (I decided to abbreviate *Assface*. He's not even worth spelling the whole name out).

Monday, July 19, 2010

I'm lonely. Anna is always talking about her new man and how much he adores her. I want that, but only from Carter. Colleen is always talking about her boyfriend saving up money for an engagement ring. I want that, but only from Carter. I've already been proposed to twice, and each time, all I could think about was why it wasn't Carter asking me.

After my voice lesson today, I sat and gossiped with my teacher, Nora, for a good hour and a half. I was talking for most of the hour, telling Carter stories, and had barely touched the tip of the iceberg. By the time I finished what I was saying, I was exhausted and drained, not because I was talking too much but because his presence in my life takes a toll on me. He really takes my breath away. Literally.

After my brief disclosure session with her, she too was worn out. "What a story you have there, Lily. I can't wait until you write that book. I want to know the whole story. I'm on the edge of my seat, wanting to know what's next and what was before," she said with sheer curiosity.

Call it a sixth sense if you must, but I have a knack for picking up love and relationship auras. I always thought it was just an intensely accurate gut feeling, but Nora was adamant that I'm a clairsentient. (Someone who can sense and understand the intensity of emotions very well).

The second I met Carter, I knew that we would be a part of each other's lives forever, in whatever capacity that meant. I don't believe in love at first sight, but I do believe in connection at first sight.

The simple glance he gave me upon first seeing me from across the parking lot was enough to turn my world upside down. On his end, I sensed an immediate and immense desire for him to be near me. That was ten years ago, and true to my intuition, we are still very much a part of each other's lives.

My visceral feeling—and now I'm more confident about it, thanks to Nora since she confirmed my ability—is telling me that he will come back to me. I'd rather not wait, but I trust my gut so much that I'm willing to stay single for the chance to be with him later.

My love connection spotting skills started before my teens. I remember one particular instance at the age of twelve.

I said what I thought without thinking of the implications my words would have later on in life. During a Christmas party at our house, my cousin Nora (not my voice teacher) was talking to a family friend whom she had just recently met.

I took one look at the two of them engrossed in conversation and immediately told my mom that they were going to get married. My mom brushed off my comment and said that I was being silly. Nora was already engaged to be married.

Sure enough, many years down the road, Nora got divorced and got married to Max, the guy I had originally and blatantly seen as her life partner. At their wedding, my mom remembered my comment from years before and asked me how I knew. I told her I just knew.

I can't explain how I knew. I just felt it. It was easy to see. She begged to differ. Not one single person had ever suspected a connection between Max and Nora. Things like that happen to me all the time. I can never explain how I know. I *just* know.

So, I'm telling you, I just *know* that Carter and I are meant to be together, but I don't know when. That's a problem because it's torture.

Tuesday, July 20, 2010

He's online all the time. Why is he torturing me? I want that carrot. He's slowly becoming the elephant in the room. I can't do anything about him, but he's always there. I would never wish this life on anyone. Truly.

Wednesday, July 21, 2010

Carter Swinton! Carter Swinton! Carter Swinton! I was trying all day to telepathically send him messages to make him contact me just so I could hear his "special" text tone and see his name scroll across my cell phone screen.

I definitely had a dream about him last night, and it wasn't to my liking. That much I remember. Unfortunately, I don't remember the details, or maybe it was fortunate since it wasn't going my way anyway.

One of my previous students e-mailed me and made it absolutely clear that I am her inspiration and role model. She essentially wants to be me and live my lifestyle.

Why can't I inspire Carter like that? Everyone else and their mothers and fathers seem to find me an anomaly in today's society. The fact that I have brains, beauty, passion, and, most importantly, God in my life is a rarity that others appreciate in me.

Carter! Appreciate me. Could it be that he appreciates me too much, and it scares him, or is this me rationalizing his absence from my life?

It's times like these that it's hard for me to believe that God never takes without giving something in return, that when God shuts one door, He opens another. I can't find the other door!! Where is it?

Thursday, July 22, 2010

Today started off on the right foot, with no sign of Carter at all. As the day progressed, I was excited that Carter didn't come up at all. This was a monumental day.

It was 10:00 p.m., and still no sign of Carter. I thought I was home free. All I had to do was get ready for bed and sleep. I hadn't talked about him all day. My thoughts were another story. Baby steps. That's all I ask.

But of course, the stars didn't align for me tonight, and today had to include Carter. I got a last minute phone call to hold an emergency tutoring session. Little did I know that my personal, self-appointed, private, undercover detective (the lady who used to live in Manhattan Beach) also needed to have an emergency conversation with me about Carter.

The first words out of her mouth when I arrived tonight, "Let me see some more pictures of Carter. I need to make sure I'm looking for the right guy," she brazenly requested. I showed her the pictures I had on my phone, only to have her reiterate what I already knew; Carter is *hot*. *I miss my hot Carter.*

Then she notably mentioned that she went to Manhattan Beach last weekend and looked for Carter but didn't see him. I appreciated the information, I really did, but what had I gotten myself into? Even people who didn't know him were intertwined in my story.

When I got home from the emergency tutoring session, I went through my mail. I got a letter with a gift inside. Under normal circumstances, any girl would be excited and thrilled, but I wasn't.

It was from Drake, a nineteen-year-old boy I met on my trip to Israel a few months ago, who was absolutely in love with me. He was traveling with friends and thought of me when he saw the handmade pottery trinket with my horoscope, a Scorpio symbol, painted on it. It was very intricately made; it was a neat gift, I thought as I tossed it into my drawer of oblivion.

The letter mentioned that even though we didn't talk much, I was still on his mind. Any girl would have died reading those words, but not me, because it wasn't from Carter.

But, I suppose there is a reason why Carter and I aren't talking at this point in life. My two best friends are obsessed with the men in their lives and need someone levelheaded to keep them in check. Since Carter and I aren't talking, which means he's only occupying a third of my brain capacity instead of three quarters of it, I am as sane as I'll ever get.

On the one hand, Colleen was obsessed with the notion that she was pregnant even though she'd never even had sex with her boyfriend. On the other hand, Anna was obsessed with her college professor, whom she just met weeks before. They were both too excited or anxious to listen to the other one; they just wanted to talk.

Clearly, they couldn't discuss these issues with each other. So I ended up being their therapist, which I had plenty of background in.

I know I have a great head on my shoulders, except for this one chink in my armor: Carter Swinton.

I suppose this journaling that I'm doing is healthy and keeping me out of depression, but I just don't know how to make him Houdini out of my life.

The permanent overarching question that looms over my head like a stormy rain cloud that follows only me—"How do I make you vanish from my life, Carter Swinton?"—is causing such sorrow in my life. Oh, Carter, look what you've done to me.

Friday, July 23, 2010

I took a half day from work to go to the beach with Rico, the ex-boyfriend. All morning, I was excited; but during the drive to his house in Seal Beach, I started to feel guilty.

I know how in love he is with me and how not in love with him I am. I love him, I really do, just not the same way he does. He would do *anything* for me, but I don't feel strongly enough to reciprocate that kind of love.

Poor guy, I'm torturing him. I'm giving him hope when, in fact, I want nothing more than a friendship from him. But of course, being Lily, I don't know how *not* to flirt around guys, so he's totally getting the wrong idea.

I ended up staying the night, and the entire night, all I could think about was how much I wanted to be at Carter's place, not

Rico's. It's not that I don't enjoy Rico's company. It's just that I enjoy Carter's company *that* much more.

Saturday, July 24, 2010

I went to my friend, Veronica's, wedding in Redondo Beach. Do you realize how close that is to Manhattan Beach? It's just a hop and a skip away.

I tried convincing my family to drive by AF's house before the reception and again after the reception, to no avail. They said I was being silly for even entertaining that thought.

I've known Veronica for most of my life and have known how awkward she used to be. She's a year younger than me, but somehow she managed to find a good-looking man, who happens to be a lawyer (Carter has hope) who sees the light of the world through her eyes.

I usually love weddings, but today I was bitter. I felt sorry for myself and angry with Assface. I was sad that he wasn't with me. I wanted him with me and felt an emptiness physically and mentally. I was very distracted during the ceremony and didn't cry at all, which was a first. I always cry at weddings out of happiness. Today, I avoided eye contact with the bride and groom for fear of raining on their parade with my bad attitude.

Unbeknownst to myself, during the speeches, I was making very sarcastic and mocking sounds that my friend, sitting at the table with me, commented on afterward. I was not in the mood for a wedding today.

It felt like I went to a wedding or baby shower at least once a month, and I was really starting to become a jealous person. Life would be so much easier if we all had the names of our other half etched into the bottom of our feet, just like Woody from *Toy Story*.

The best part about the wedding wasn't the wedding itself. It was the fact that I was seated next to an old friend at the reception. I was truly excited to see her. The first thing out of her mouth was, "How's Carter? That's his name, right?" Oh, my word. I really do tell everyone. I should just assume that everyone knows. The odds would be better to assume that everyone in my life knows something about AF rather than not.

So there I was, updating her on the new developments in my Carter Swinton saga and getting the same reaction from her as everyone else—sheer amazement in the long-drawn-out drama. One day I'll be telling my Carter story with a happy ending. I just hope that day comes sooner rather than later.

It's standard that every wedding I go to I make a new friend or two. It was no surprise that I met a girl whom I had an instant connection with, who, by the end of the night, was trying to set me up with one of her friends.

She was describing her friend as a tall, dark, and handsome orthodontist who lives by the beach; and to any girl, he would sound absolutely delectable. But all I could think was *I don't really want to meet him because he's not Carter*, which seemed to be my motto these days.

I should just write a country song and have the chorus be, "Because he's not Carter." I say that or think that almost every second of every day.

Sunday, July 25, 2010

I wasn't happy today. I had Carter withdrawals. Even worse, my sister came into my room crying over a boy. Her story scarily resembled my Carter saga.

Of all the things to learn from a big sister, she had to learn how to become attached to the wrong boys. I've failed at my duties as a big sister. I should be fired.

Still, I couldn't help but laugh out loud when she said, "I don't want to be with anyone if I'm not going to love him like I love Randy, because I know what it feels like to love someone intensely." I laughed because just a few years ago, those were my *exact* words. I thought kids were supposed to take after their parents, not their siblings.

My mom's biggest issue with Carter right now (she changes her mind often) is that he believes Christianity is a big hoax. To her, that reason alone is enough for me to drop him and find a new love.

But, what if we looked at Carter and me using an analogy? We are both the lens on a projector seeing the same image on the screen. However, my image is more focused, sharp, and clear because of my relationship with God. His image, on the other hand, is fuzzy and blurred because it is out of focus.

We both believe in a higher being, but my belief is much stronger, so I have clarity and direction in my life. His image lacks direction but can easily be corrected with an adjustment of the lens.

All hope is not lost on Carter. It is doubtful that he will make that adjustment on his own without an extreme event happening in his life, but it is possible. He just may be the one-in-a-million statistic that I'm hoping for.

Monday, July 26, 2010

Carter is such a wank. I like that word. It has just the right amount of derogatory without being too inappropriate, and includes a tinge of humor.

That wank's Facebook profile is constantly updated with pictures of himself showing off. I remember, in college, going to a guy's room and seeing posed pictures of himself posted up all over his room. I was turned off quicker than you could say "eww."

Now, here I was fawning over a man, who's still a boy, who had nothing better to do than post pictures of himself online (public domain).

I do the same thing but only for Carter's benefit. On my Facebook, I love to post pictures that show off my body, my athleticism, and the fact that I have many good-looking male friends who I spend time with. All my pictures are posted for Carter's benefit, and no one else's. The irony of the situation was not lost on me.

The only difference between Carter and me is that I don't write anything in my status to show off. I'm just a sneaky show off, just like the rest of my nature. God definitely has a sense of humor and a way of turning life into pure entertainment.

Tuesday, July 27, 2010

Would you leave a lover to be with your soul mate? It seems as though most people are afraid of having a sincerely deep connection with another person. I, on the other hand, long for that connection with such a yearning desire. I would rather wait a lifetime for that soul mate than end up with the wrong person. Carter Swinton is my soul mate. I am foolishly loyal to this undeserving wanker. It never dawned on me that my foolish behavior comes from my role model.

Unfortunately, my mom is loyal to a tee. She is in the process of a much-needed divorce from my dad, yet she wavers and thinks that maybe she could try again. She moved out three years ago, but now she thinks that maybe she could come back and, at the very least, live civilly with my dad, without love and romance. I can't say that I'm completely responsible for how I am. I have definitely made a case for the argument between nature and nurture.

My mom says that I will never find another man if I don't make myself an empty vessel. I need to be brave enough to say good-bye in order to be rewarded with a new hello. I need to clean out my system to give God room to guide me. Without

God's guidance, my life will not have any purpose, and I will ultimately live a sad and lonely life.

Wednesday, July 28, 2010

I woke up in an interesting mood. I had a dream about the epitome of a jerk ex-boyfriend, Dan (for once it wasn't about Carter), and saw that I had a few text messages from Reed, the childhood friend I went out on a date with. I thought he wasn't interested. I guess he was. He said he wanted to get dinner again. That made me smile.

Thursday, July 29, 2010

Carter's status message was a topic of conversation for me today with at least a dozen friends. He had a link that facetiously described the way student loans work.

I so badly wanted to message him and tell him that I almost had a stroke reading it. It was that funny. But that would be counterproductive.

He had the link posted for attention. He wanted people to comment on it. I won't give him what he wants. He needs to start giving me attention. In the meantime, I'll just enjoy his posts from a distance. Maybe one day I'll be able to tell him that I enjoyed his posts and that they brought levity to my day.

Reed and I talked for a while. He mentioned how busy he was going to be on the weekend, but that he would make time to have dinner with me. He also said that he wanted to come support me in my mud run in a few weeks. He wanted to be there to cheer me on.

Now this is what a guy is supposed to do if he wants your company. He needs to make an effort to be in your presence. Why can't that jackass Carter do that?

Friday, July 30, 2010

Today, Yelena, one of my math students, came in to make up a test. After finishing her math test, and passing, of course, she randomly asked me if I was still writing my book. I completely forgot that I told her about Carter and my plans of "the book."

I really should just assume everyone knows. I can't control myself when it comes to that boy. She ended up giving me advice and counseling me. Mind you, she's only seventeen, but she had some pretty mature insight.

She was asking me who I thought was smarter, me or him. I said we are smart in different areas, but if I had to choose, I would say he's smarter.

I told her about his non-question texts, and she said, "Oh, then he is very smart. He's not asking you any questions because he knows you aren't going to respond and doesn't want to be rejected. He's just confused right now. He'll come back to you."

Not a single one of my other friends gave me that insight. If I were younger, this girl would be my best friend. I love her. She's a smart girl. Many of my students had gotten pregnant at a young age. That won't happen to Yelena. She's too smart for that.

My long-time friend, Jaylin, called to catch up. I hadn't spoken with her in a while and I updated her on Carter because she asked. I mentioned the journaling I was doing for my soul and that I wanted to turn it into a book. At that point, she reminded me about the Easter story that she insisted I include in the book. Done.

Everyone has a favorite Carter story. I should just take requests. I doubt I'll ever have a shortage of people to tell the story to because as soon as I tell the story to someone, there are new developments in the saga for me to be able to go through my rounds again.

This was a dangerous cycle, never letting go of him. Carter was a lifestyle for me. I wouldn't know what to do without him in my life.

On the other hand, Randy, my sister's guy, was just a habit, which is why she was able to get over him. Carter had been in my life for ten years, while Randy had been in my sister's life for only three years. That was a big difference.

Out of curiosity, I looked up Carter's tenth-year high school reunion information. He was ASB president, so he was in charge of organizing the event. Turns out his reunion is tomorrow night at a hotel in Los Angeles at 7:30 p.m.

I needed someone to invite me to go hang out there. I wanted to randomly run into him. Would that be considered stalking if I took a friend and just hung out there on the off chance that I might run into him? I know there are no guarantees, but I'm willing to sacrifice an evening just to be near him.

Saturday, July 31, 2010

I have not woken up in this wonderful of a mood for a long, long time. My heart was beating so fast, and I was beaming. I had the most amazing dream about Carter. It had been a while since I vividly dreamt about him and enjoyed the entire dream. There were so many aspects to this dream that made me more hopeful for the future.

> I am hanging out with some friends, Carter included. Since we haven't been on speaking terms for a while, we were ignoring each other. Out of nowhere, he says, "You never gave me a valentine." It's months after Valentine's Day. It's quite an irrelevant comment. I happen to be eating dried fruit, and find a piece of fruit that is shaped like a heart,

and I give it to him. He is unusually appreciative of the simple gesture.

Accusingly, I say, "You never gave me a valentine." I am expecting some excuse or blame as usual; instead, he reaches into his back pocket and pulls out a heart-shaped candle. I couldn't help but say "Awww." I am genuinely touched. He goes on to say, "I bought it on my way here from a shop off Pico Boulevard. The workers were strange, the shop smelled funny, and I felt like I could have been in danger, but I really wanted to get you something." I am truly touched. He makes it a point to tell me that he went to great lengths to get me that heart-shaped candle. He leaves the room to go use the bathroom. In the meantime, his friends pull out a letter that he had written and started reading it to me. It was a long, convoluted letter, but it basically stated that the last girl he sees before he leaves (he is leaving for Australia the next day and will stay there for six months) is the girl he has intense feelings for. This is the girl he loves and wants to spend the rest of his life with. I am confused. Was this letter meant for me? Carter comes back into the room, and we are both silent. We all decide to go for a walk outside. He comes over to me and starts walking backward so that he is facing me. We just gaze into each other's eyes. I break the silence. "Do you really love me?" He softly says, "Yes, I do. I'm sorry for being stupid. I really do care about you." We embrace tightly, kiss passionately, and cry freely. I try to lighten up the mood by asking, "You really didn't like that I was mean to you and ignored you for the last couple of months, did you?" With a smile on his face, he says, "Not at all, but I deserved it." I say, "You're leaving tomorrow for six months." He says, "I won't forget you. I'll be back for you." I say, "I'll be waiting right here for you."

Meanwhile, our friends are surrounding us, witnessing this spectacular moment, which is deserving of fireworks.

This was the first dream in the ten years that I've known Carter where he proclaimed his love for me in public. For once, I wasn't the secret girlfriend or the girl on the side that no one knew about. He was finally serious.

I don't claim to be psychic or to be a prophet, but I trust my dreams the same way I trust my gut feelings. I dream with intense feeling that I cannot deny.

The first thing I did this morning was call my best friend, Anna, to tell her about the dream. She was so emotional, she cried. The dream itself was filled with emotion, let alone the history that it stemmed from. I immediately called my mom afterward, and she cried as well.

Everyone has a stake in this story. Everyone has a vested interest in this story. Everyone wants me to finally have my dream come true. Everyone wants me to just be happy.

I told my sister the story as well, and she asked me what my interpretation was. Like a silly, giddy girl, I said, "I think Carter is finally realizing how precious a commodity I am."

She started laughing hysterically. "You really think that because you had the dream, he is going to start shaping up? That doesn't even make sense. He doesn't even know you had the dream," she mockingly said.

I suppose she's right. However, she also doesn't understand how my dreams work. Somehow, when I have truly intense dreams, as this one was, they turn into reality. I'm not saying that the dream will come true but that there is some truth to what I intensely felt and experienced in my dream. It's almost as if I've picked up some energy subconsciously.

I said, "Okay, realistically, I think the dream symbolizes that even when I think he's ready to be with me, I will still have to wait. He declared his love for me, but the catch was I had to wait six months. The six months could also symbolize the extent of how much he can tolerate that lame trophy girlfriend of his before he gets bored and returns to the real jewel—me."

Dreams are fantastic. I had a great day today.

I don't claim to be psychic at all. I feel like God has given me a gift of being in tune with the energies of the world. I truly believe that there is a reason for every creation and every action. If I didn't have this insight or glimpse into the future, I might go crazy. God knows this and therefore gave me this gift.

Sunday, August 1, 2010

"Anna! Do you think I'm psycho for believing the dream I had last night will come true?" I imploringly asked Anna first thing in the morning.

She had such a way with her words, delicately reproaching me. "You're a very strong-willed woman; you know what you want and go after it until you get it. You're adamant about getting what you think you deserve. But, for some strange reason, you feel like you deserve this Assface, so I have no doubt that you will stop at nothing, including believing your dreams will become a reality. Sticking to your gut feeling doesn't equate to psycho for me, but it might to others. Just be careful who you share your thoughts with, Lily."

It's a little too late to be careful; the whole world knows about Carter.

My sister and I made a realization today. I'm having a very difficult time getting over Carter because I was so convinced that we would be together at this point in my life, so now I was mourning the death of the life I thought I would have. I wasn't able to simply exist in my memorable moments with Carter; I was now living in their shadows.

I went to Carter Movelli's (Carter Swinton's twin) house today. He had a group of his law school classmates over. As I was watching them interact with each other, the chemistry between them and the close bonds made me sick to my stomach. To know that at one point, Carter Swinton was this close to a group of friends made me queasy. I wanted to be part of the in crowd with Carter!

Instantaneously, I became jealous of Carter Swinton's friends, who I knew nothing of, simply because they had the opportunity to spend time with him.

Despite my negative vibe, I got hit on by three very good-looking males, yet I was in no mood to be enchanted. They weren't Carter.

Monday, August 2, 2010

While I was wallowing in my lonely misery, I unwisely decided to take a look at Carter's Facebook. All I did was fuel my melancholy mood. It was plastered with pictures from his high school reunion on Saturday.

He took that stupid blonde with him. She was wearing his suit coat. They were close in every picture *and* worst of all, he looked really happy. His smiles were genuine. They really, really liked each other. This was a sad, sad day. The future is looking bleak for him and me.

For the entire month of July, I gave up sweets and bread, just because. I had no reason to give myself such restrictions, but I liked the challenge, and it ended up being fairly easy for me. Maybe that's why I like Carter so much; a challenge I can't defeat.

Since the food challenge wasn't difficult enough, maybe this month should be giving up Carter Swinton. There's no way I can give him up in thought or heart, but I can give him up in conversation and on the computer (checking his Facebook and his Gmail status).

After thinking about it, it crossed my mind that I might be holding the bar too high for myself. Maybe I'll start by giving him up for one week.

I also don't like to fail at my own challenges, so let's be realistic here and give myself an attainable goal. If I do well, then I can up the ante.

Tuesday, August 3, 2010

I officially gave him up, starting today, and I did very well. Every time I wanted to talk about him, I bit my tongue and silently talked to myself. I can't believe how often I would *make* him part of my conversation. This will be very good for me. If I can do this, I can do *anything*.

Wednesday, August 4, 2010

The second day of breaking a habit is always easier. There were many opportunities for me to bring him up, and I didn't. I didn't scroll down my Gchat list to see if he was online or check his Facebook. I know it's only been two days, but I have to praise myself for any progress I made in the Carter department, as small as it may be.

Although, he did pop up in my friend update on Facebook because he commented on someone's status, and I was forced to read it. He said that he would be flying to Texas over Labor Day weekend, and that he hoped his friends would be in town so he could see them.

This worried me. What if he was going on a mini vacation with his blonde chick, Brook, and hoping that his friends were in town so that he could show her off? Isn't he tired of her yet?

This might actually be more serious than I thought. Wait! I just checked her team's dance schedule. She's supposed to be in Cinncinnati, Ohio, on Labor Day weekend. Maybe he really does just want to see his friends. Phew! I just majorly wiped some sweat off my brow.

Most people who believe in God would wonder why God has forsaken them when they don't get their way, why He isn't answering their prayers. At times it truly is difficult to have complete faith in Him and not worry. But, I truly believe in the power of prayer and the power of God. I *know* that God will not give me anything I can't handle. I just wish He didn't trust me so much. Can't He see that I've gone on for ten years without making any head-way? I think it's time for Him to step in and take over.

I also know that there is a reason for *everything* that happens. I realize that I have freewill and that I have choices in my life path, but ultimately God is always around, watching, hoping that I pick up on His guidance and make the choices that help me live out my faith best. That's where I have trouble: discernment. I *know* what the right thing to do is in most cases, but I can rationalize any argument to death, just to make it seem right in my mind.

I knew what doing the right thing looked like: giving up Carter Swinton. Often times, what we want to do and what we have to do are not the same. My mommy told me once that the tighter the space between my desire and what is right, the happier I'll be. My desire wasn't right; it was all wrong.

For the last ten years, I existed in my perception of us together and now I didn't want to admit that I had nothing. I felt like Jay Gatsby, swooning over Daisy, years after meeting and having her tumble short of his dreams, not because there was anything wrong with her, but because of the vitality of his illusion of her.

All the grandeur and sparkle I stored up in my mind was no match for the real Carter Swinton, who would always fall short of my image of him. I suppose God was answering my prayers. A life with Carter would never amount to the life I've created for us within the dark crevices of my mind.

Thursday, August 5, 2010

No big news today. I suppose that's a good thing.

Friday, August 6, 2010

"I want you to want me, I need you to need me," the song lyrics came to mind as I restlessly woke up from yet another dream about Carter.

Ironically, while those lyrics were running through my mind, I was thinking of ways to get revenge.

Now, instead of looking for ways to run into him, my mind looked for ways to get back at him. Could I slash his tires? Na, too much like the movies. Should I get ahold of Brook and tell her all about Carter? Nope, that's too petty. Would I be daring enough to go to his house and slap him? Not a chance.

No matter what I thought of, nothing seemed fitting enough to give me the satisfaction I desired. The problem is that revenge is not fulfilling. Revenge is a poison *you* take hoping the other person will die.

Saturday, August 7, 2010

I went to Rico's house today, the ex-boyfriend. All night, while we were cuddling, I was imagining that he was Carter. Thank goodness Rico couldn't read my mind. I guess the saying, "If you want to know where your heart is, look to where your mind goes when it wanders," is true. It just wants what it wants.

Sunday, August 8, 2010

Even worse, I slept next to him and dreamt about Carter. Clearly, my heart was not with Rico at all. Not that this was news to me. I just really thought that I was finally starting to clear my mind of Carter. So much for wanting revenge; that was a short-lived idea.

I met Brook, the blonde girlfriend, and she was crying. I comforted her, and I ended up liking her. She was crying because she got laid off from her job as a beach volleyball cheerleader. Because she got laid off, Carter broke up with her. Apparently, he was only with her because of her job. I really did feel bad for her, but I knew it was bound to happen. I was immediately cut into another scene where only Carter and I were in a room. He wouldn't look at me, and when I would look at him and catch him staring, he would turn away. Instead of talking to me, he kept on texting me. He was asking me how I've been, and if we could hang out.

I remember that I was angry with him in my dream.

Why do I always have to be the backup girl? I realize that I'm the most quality girl out there for him, and he knows that. Even my subconscious knows that. But how long must I wait for this jackass to crawl out of his funk?

I left Rico's place and spent the rest of the day with Ray, another ex-boyfriend. On the way, I drove on the 110, which is the way to drive to USC, where Carter went to college. I've driven that freeway very often and know the twists and turns like the back of my hand. There is one particular turn, right before Stadium Way that has a dangerous dip.

One day, when I was driving on the 110 to visit other friends of mine who attended USC, he called me right as I was driving on this dip. I almost got into an accident because I got so excited that Carter Swinton's name was scrolling across my cell phone.

The combination of the dip, which to this day still exists and stirs up that memory, and the excitement of him calling me was enough to make my stomach flutter and make me lose control of my car for a brief moment. Every time I drive right by that spot, I can't help but be reminded of that glorious almost catastrophe, get a few butterflies in my stomach, and a smile on my face.

I don't know that I can admit to having very fond memories of anything that doesn't involve Carter. The second you add him into the equation, then it constitutes a memory worth keeping. So sad, Lily. So sad.

Monday, August 9, 2010

I wore jeans to work today; a pair of perfectly worn in jeans I've had for over ten years. A little outdated, these jeans had pockets at the bottom where they flare out, and the waist was so high. Well, maybe a lot outdated, but every time I cleaned out my closet, I just couldn't bear to give them away because of the vivid recollection attached to them, like a nagging stain.

When I first met Carter ten years ago, I wore these jeans, also out of style back then. I clearly remember the comment he made about them, and because of that single memory, I'm forever stuck with the jeans.

He positioned one leg on the bench, elbow on his knee, leaned closer toward me and amusingly asked, "What exactly would you carry in that pocket? It's so inconvenient." Then he mocked me, bent over, and in a grotesquely high pitched voice said, "Excuse me while I bend down to get something out of my pocket."

To this day, I can't help but crack a smile every time I think of him saying that to me. The problem is, memories like this make it difficult to annihilate my desire for Carter. I don't want to want him so much that it becomes part of my chemical makeup.

Since it's more feasible to accept that I won't get over him, I'll just imagine that one day, when we are married, I'll wear the jeans for him and he'll see the humor in that.

So when I turned to my computer and saw an instant message from him, I was overwhelmed. The combination of the jeans and his message flustered me. It's more Carter action than I've had in a while. I was both excited and shocked.

Carter: hi, I went to a great place that u might like
Me: where
Carter: Hesperia
Me: ha...why would I like it?
Carter: I hiked to these natural hot mineral springs in the
    middle of a canyon in the middle of nowhere and it's
    "tan-line optional"
Me: cool...what's it called so I can go?
    two and a half hours later...
Carter: it's called deep creek. wanted to say hi I guess.

There are so many things to ponder about this conversation, if you can even call it that. It really got me thinking. This boy makes me feel so conflicted, and my emotions run amuck. Within seconds, I'm about to burst, intoxicated with elation immediately to sober up to disappointment and dejection. I'm always torn between multiple emotions with him.

After this talk, I was upset with myself for buckling and responding to him, but I was also ecstatic that he still had me on his mind and messaged me. My mind was a whirlwind of thoughts. First of all, I failed at not responding to him. I gave in. That really pissed me off. He won again.

The second I responded, it was the same feeling you get when you click on those links in your e-mail that say, "I found these pictures of you, click to see," only to realize that it was sent to you by someone you haven't spoken to in years (there's no reason for them to have pictures of you) and that it's a virus.

Instantaneously, you know that your curiosity got the better of you and got you into trouble.

That's exactly how I felt answering Carter. I knew it was wrong to respond, but I did. I was just that curious. He tried a new tactic, and it worked. On the other hand, he tried a *new* tactic. (He's thinking about ways to communicate with me). He's not done with me, not by a long shot. A hint of a smile flickered across my face as it dawned on me that maybe he's a homing pigeon and I'm his home.

I knew that this boy always had ulterior motives. I had gotten good at figuring out what they were. This time there were two; he wanted to see if his new tactic would work, and he wanted to show off that he does fun activities.

I truly appreciate that he offered me the information because I do love hiking, and I will explore this hike; but it also upsets me because I don't know if he went with the chick, and I despise thinking about him and her together. *Ugh. Leave already, blonde chick! You're stealing my man!*

I was so overwhelmed with emotions that I cried. The problem is I never know why I'm crying. Is it because Carter talked to me? Because Brook is still in his life? Because I'm constantly wavering on a fine line of love and hate? Because I want to hike with him? Because I love him so much? Is it the fact that I'm missing out on small moments with Carter or is it the bigger picture that tugs at my tear ducts? It's an unsolvable mystery. I've been on the case for ten years and haven't made any headway.

By the way, I failed at my one-week Carter fast. Two days into it, I should have been fired.

Did you notice how long it took him to tell me the name of the hike after I asked? At first, I thought he forgot about me, and then I looked at the situation through the eyes of the asshole. He was making a statement: "You're on my time." It was almost two and a half hours later when he finally gave me an answer.

I'm almost positive that he did that on purpose, that he knew I'd ask about the hike, but never intended on responding in a timely manner. He wanted to know that he still held the reins to my emotions. How easily I handed them over to him, trusting that he would lead me in the right direction this time.

Tuesday, August 10, 2010

Ahhh! I'm in a good mood today simply because of that short conversation. It revealed so much to me. I'm so easily excitable. I'm too easy to please when it comes to Stupid Boy. I'm stuck in love.

I went to my friend Marissa's house after work and had dinner with her and, of course, caught her up to speed with my Other Life (the Carter-inundated life). She gave me some insights that I already knew and some that I didn't want to believe. It's always nice to be reassured of what you already know. Funny how hearing what I want to hear becomes fact in my mind. Yet hearing information that disagrees with my thoughts *can't* be true.

She mentioned that on the day I ran into him on the beach, it was very possible that he actually went down to the beach in hopes of running into me, which was why he probably texted me earlier that day. He wanted to make sure I was in the vicinity so he would know where to look for me. I like that.

She also said that he is for sure going to come back to me after he's done with this blonde toy—whom he cares nothing for—at least not for the long term. He may have gotten with her to show her off at the reunion. He knew his ten-year high school reunion was right around the corner and needed a hot party chick to show off, not an intellectual like me. I didn't like that.

If he is really that sneaky and calculated, I would truly be disappointed. That's too conniving for me. Even that is beneath me, and a lot of things are not beneath me when it comes to shadiness and getting what I want with Carter. But would I be too disappointed to take him back if he so decided? Not at all. I'd wanted Carter for so long, I didn't even remember what it was like not to.

Wednesday, August 11, 2010

I got three texts this morning from three different guys all telling me "good morning." All three of these guys are totally interested and willing to give me the world, and I don't want it from them, because they're not Carter. Sing it with me now: "Because he's not Carter."

I had a date at 5:30 this evening. He arrived at 6:30 p.m. I didn't care that he was late because I wasn't even excited about the date. Don't get me wrong, Jeff (whom I met at my ex-boyfriend's son's first birthday party) is a great guy, and I enjoyed his company, but not the same way he enjoyed mine.

He was ready to drop down on his knees and propose to me-I could see it in his eyes. I told him as soon as I got in the car, "Don't fall in love with me. It's harder than you think." He didn't believe me.

During the entire hour Jeff was late fighting traffic, I was talking to my sister about none other than the curse on my life, Carter. My sister walked into my room and found me standing there, staring at a calendar that hung from my hands. "What are you doing?" she asked in a laughing manner. "Every time I see you, you're doing something ridiculous."

I said with conviction, "I'm investigating. Investigating Carter. I would be an excellent private investigator. I'm finding out lots of stuff." Instead of being nervous, or even excited, for my date, I was concentrating on digging up information on Carter and checking out his Facebook. So here's what I found:

> May 13: Carter went to Downtown Disney for a networking event for work and posted a picture of the entrance to Downtown Disney on Facebook.
> June 9: Carter broke up with me.
> June 27: Blondie commented on his Downtown Disney Facebook picture. She wrote, "Thank God for this

night." *This means that's where they met, and it also means she really likes him and is plastering that all over the web. Tacky in my opinion.*

July 5: Carter posted on his Facebook, "The Master said, is goodness indeed so far away? If we really wanted goodness, we should find that it is at our very side." *The Analects of Confucius*

On that same day, Brook wrote underneath a picture of them together: "Pretty sure this is what Confucius is talking about." *Again, showing too much neediness on a public domain.*

July 31: After Carter's ten-year reunion, the chick posted on his Facebook wall, "Thank you for tonight! XO." *These are private messages. Is anyone else in agreement with me?*

August 11: *Today* He posted a comment on Chick's bikini picture on the beach. "Beautiful," he wrote. *I never thought I'd see the day when he would write that word on public domain. That's too much into his private life. I'm not going to lie, this makes me nervous. Maybe he really does like her. It also makes me sad because I've dreamt countless times of him telling me I'm beautiful, and never has he called me beautiful. Now he's labeling this girl he doesn't even care about (now I'm not so sure) with the word that's supposed to be meant for me—beautiful. I'm jealous. Is that okay? I can't help it. She's living the life I want to live.*

Here are my thoughts in a nutshell. They are both enthralled and infatuated with each other for the time being. He is enthralled with her beauty, which will fade and become boring to him in time if she doesn't have the personality and intellect to uphold the looks.

She is enthralled with him, in general. I mean, who wouldn't be? He's a hot commodity. She really likes him, but he will eventually get fed up with her neediness, at least that's what I'm hoping will happen.

Let's look at this logically. There is no way he can spend the rest of his life with a cheerleader. He can't marry a woman like that to raise his kids. That's just obnoxious. Where are the core values? I bet she's not a smartass like I am, and I know he likes that about me. He'll get bored with her blasé personality, which exudes from her Facebook pictures. I'm sure she doesn't have much depth to her. He'll be in lust for a while though.

It's really going to test my patience, but I know it, I just know it; he'll be back for me. Even this jackass can't help but fall in love with me. He can't deny how great I am even though he wants to. He's said it multiple times. I'm the goodness and sweetness in his life. He asks himself, "What would Lily do in this situation?" He looks up to me.

For some reason, he doesn't want to like me, but he *really* does. My mom says it's because I am light and he is dark. The light in me scares him away, yet it attracts him to me.

I get up at 5:30 every morning to do my *Insanity* workout, and right now, I'm journaling at 1:48 a.m. I'm insane. I'm willing to give up my sleep to write about Carter, yet I'm not willing to lose sleep to spend time with friends. My sleep is a priority with friends and family, but with Carter, even on paper, he's the priority. I'm a maniac, but he makes me like that. My head is definitely screwed on backward.

Thursday, August 12, 2010

I feel like I'm married to Carter. I'm so committed that I can't open up my heart to anyone else. At least that's what my mommy tells me.

I like to look at the situation from a different perspective. I am a very sexual being, and I need somewhere to channel my energy. If I weren't that committed to him, I feel like I could very well have been a major slut.

God is gracing me with Carter, not torturing me. That's what people don't understand. Carter Swinton is a blessing in my life. He's keeping me from being a bad girl.

He's getting more aggressive now. He's instant-messaging me more often and finding new tactics to get me to respond. They're working.

> Carter: ur insane?
> *In regard to my Gchat post: "Insanity rocks my world."*
> Me: *I sent him the link to the 60-day workout DVDs called Insanity.*
> Carter: easy-peasy P90x wasn't enough?
> *He's talking about a 90 day workout DVD set that I had completed earlier.*
> Me: I like this better
> *I'm trying as best as I can to be short with him.*
> Carter: ohhh...I want that. I just started reading a new book the other day
> Me: ?
> Carter: the new testament
> *In the Bible, if you remember, this is where we had our disagreements, because he doesn't believe it's valid, whereas I do.*
> It's a pretty good fairy tale
> *He's totally trying to be funny and make conversation with me.*

So, it's clear to me that he's still very interested. It's obvious that I don't want to talk to him, yet he is making a major effort to carry on a conversation. He is almost monologueing (I may have made that word up, but it works) online, which I find somewhat embarrassing for him.

If he truly didn't care, he would drop the conversation. What he's doing is a lot of work, work he shouldn't be doing if he has a girlfriend. He's making sure I know that he still cares. He knows that I understand that. We get each other. We both know that we get each other. I just have to wait for him to get out of his little-boy phase. Hopefully, he doesn't want to be Peter Pan forever.

I had my second date of the week today. I went out with Parker (I met him at a party a few weeks ago) to the Los Angeles Art Walk. Every second Thursday of the month, up-and-coming artists display their work in galleries and buildings throughout Los Angeles. People from all walks of life go to this event. It's a very eccentric and eclectic activity.

The entire time, Parker was a gentleman, making sure to walk on the outside of the curb so that I was away from cars. (I love when guys do that). I was freezing, so he warmed me up by rubbing my arms. He held my hand at the right moment. He did everything any girl would want to happen on the first date, but here comes the chorus. "Because he's not Carter," it did *nothing* for me.

On the way home in the car, I caught myself smiling for no reason and realized that I dazed for a moment and daydreamed about Carter while I was on the date with Parker, which is so inappropriate. I'm so glad superpowers (reading minds) don't exist.

Friday, August 13, 2010

Today was my second date with Jeff (the guy from Wednesday). He came to pick me up, still dressed in slacks and a tie from work, and decided to be spontaneous and drive to the Santa Monica pier. Mind you, he'd already been driving an hour in traffic to get to my house, only to get back in the car to drive another hour in traffic to the beach.

When I mentioned that it was too much driving, he said it was absolutely worth it. I already knew where tonight was headed, and I didn't like it. I already knew from the first date that he wanted to marry me. Tonight, he actually voiced that.

I liked the guy; I just didn't want to marry him. I had to make the most of it, so we had engaging conversations in the car about religion and what you look for in a partner.

We got to the beach, walked down the pier to watch the sunset, then had dinner at Bubba Gump's, where things started to get heavy. It all started when he asked me how I knew Ray and Zoe (the husband and wife who threw the party where we met).

I knew it was going to get ugly if I was going to be utterly honest. However, the way I see it, honesty is the best policy. It may not be the easiest route, but it's the most honorable and saves heartache down the road. I chose my words carefully. "Ray was my first boyfriend," I said slowly.

"Oh," he said with a downtrodden voice. "And you're still friends."

"Yes," I said. "Most of my friends are boys. I just get along with them better. Does that bother you?"

"I'm not going to lie," he said. "Those are definitely red flags."

All I thought was, *Oh man, he's the jealous type, which is definitely not my type.* We dropped the subject and moved on to other topics. After dinner, which he paid for and would not let me contribute to, we walked around the pier and went on the Ferris wheel and some other rides. The entire time, he was holding my hand and rubbing my arms and back to keep me warm. On the Ferris wheel he sat awfully close and decided to get to the serious talk again.

"I have to tell you something," he said softly.

"You're not married or have kids or have herpes?" I asked in a worried tone. I'm such a good actress; it's really sad to see these guys fall for me while I'm just twisting the dagger in their heart even more. I know I said that honesty is the best policy, but sometimes I just can't resist. It's so easy to make someone fall in love with me, and I know all the right things to say.

Jeff said, "I'm leaving for officer school in Georgia for twelve weeks, November 17. I don't know where I'll be stationed afterwards. It might even be Germany. Is that going to be a problem?"

"That changes things," I said with a big mournful sigh, although, really, I didn't care either way. I'm not serious about him anyway. "I'm going to have to think about all this. I don't know if I can leave California," I said in a somber tone.

He then continued saying how he had no debt because the army paid for his school and tried to use that as leverage to increase his attractiveness factor to me.

"You want to move to Germany now?" he asked.

I looked at him with soft eyes, and he took that as a sign to lean in for a kiss. Damn, I'm good. I can make any guy fall for me. That bachelor's degree in psychology really did me wonders. I think I even take advantage of people unintentionally. I quickly turned my head away to dodge the kiss and said, "I don't kiss this early."

Usually, guys are taken aback by that and take a hit to their ego, but *he* found it a turn-on that I avoided the kiss. Jeff actually respected me even more. He's fallen hard. Poor guy. He had no idea what was in store for him. We got off the Ferris wheel and played some carnival games so he could try to win me a leopard stuffed animal. (I love, love, love anything leopard).

I know I brought it upon myself, but now he was throwing money on me, and I can't live with myself when people waste their hard-earned resources on me. I pulled him away from the games, and he reluctantly left empty-handed. He was so determined to win me that stuffed animal no matter how much money it took.

We then walked along the street, with him taking the side of the curb close to the street, of course. (Did I mention that I love when guys do that? It's so sweet). "Let's go to Hollywood and go to the Wax Museum," he said out of nowhere. This guy was clearly tired but didn't want to leave my company.

I had to interject. "That sounds fun, but I'm really tired. I'm sorry."

He definitely looked disappointed but respected my wishes, and we headed back to the car.

It was a long car ride home. It got *serious*. Our conversation felt like a car on the freeway, accelerating from 0 to 60 in five seconds flat. The intensity was high. We were both so tired and exhausted from a long day of work and an evening of fun. "Tell me something I don't know about you," he said.

"Okay, I've been proposed to twice. Guys fall hard for me, and I don't know why. For some reason, there is always a disconnect. I never fall quite as hard as they do. It takes a while for me to warm up to someone."

Between you, me, and this piece of paper, it's really because I have my heart guarded. It's patiently waiting for Carter Swinton to propose to me and make me Mrs. Lily Swinton. (Doesn't that have such a nice ring to it? I can't wait to change my last name).

"Are you warning me?" he asked.

"I'm just telling you something you don't know about me. Take it as you wish."

What came next was more exhausting than I could have imagined. He said, "I think we should define our relationship."

"Okay," I said. I didn't have the energy for this right now, but I guess breaking Jeff's heart when he was this invested was better done sooner rather than later.

He asked, "So what do you think about us?"

I said, "I know how serious you are, and unfortunately, I'm not at the same level of intensity as you are. I don't want you to invest your resources on someone who isn't as vested as you are. I don't want to lead you on or string you along."

"I really like you," he said. "I know what I want when I see it, and I go after it. I am dating, but I will give up everyone for you, Lily. No one compares to you. My favorite thing about you is that you're normal, so chill. (If he only knew). There is nothing wrong with you. If I had known there was a diamond in the San Gabriel Valley, I would have been out here sooner. I would love for you to be the last person I date. You are truly amazing and beautiful."

What a mouthful. He just kept rambling on (that's just what his romantic words were to me) about how great I am. You know what that did for me? *Nothing!* It actually made me angry. It made me upset because I was getting the exact attention I want from everyone *except* Carter.

We drove in silence the rest of the way home. When we got to my house, he walked me to the door, kissed my hand, and said, "If nothing comes from this, I have truly been blessed the last two days. They were two of the most amazing days I've had. It has truly been a blessing to get to know you. I think you're really great. There's no other way for me to put it. I really, really like you. If nothing romantic comes of us, I would still like to be friends, as difficult as that will be for me because I usually cut off all contact, but you are just that cool and great."

This was so heart-wrenching. I could see the tufts of heavy air rolling off his body as he spoke. I could smell the hurt and feel the pangs of pain he was going through. God, please forgive me for playing with this man's heart. I know You blessed me with very attractive characteristics inside and out, but there is no reason for me to take advantage of that and hurt others. I should be using Your gift in a positive manner.

After the long, emotionally draining evening, all I wanted to do was go to bed, but I was stopped short by my friend Max; he instant messaged me. (My Gchat is always on hoping to receive a message from Carter; I could very well be addicted).

> Max: how's it going?
> Me: I just got back from a date a bit ago...it was the second date, and he already told me he wanted me to be the last person he ever dated...basically, he wants to marry me

Max: what is with everyone trying to marry you? you're like some Rasputin or jedi mind master. You must have mystical powers or something

Me: well, when you know, you know, I guess

Max: what do you think about him?

Me: I like him, but he's not assface

Max: oh lord

Me: I'm just kidding

Max: no I don't think you are. that's the sad part

Me: haha. you're right, I'm not

Max: you should have just told him, 'Yea, I'd probably be more attracted to you if you were completely wrong for me.'

Me: haha. so sad but true. this is why I hate dating

Max: why? because you have to break things off?

Me: yes, it's stressful. because the ball is always in my court. it's never that the guy isn't interested

Max: well you did it to yourself with all your healthy eating and exercising

Me: lol that's funny

Max: it's funny because you know it's true.... if you packed on like, 50 pounds, you wouldn't be having these issues

Me: haha

Max: it's a tough world when everyone falls in love with you, I guess

Me: ha...I'm not complaining...I just feel bad like...what's wrong with me

Max: nothing. that's the problem. You need to make yourself less desirable, I suppose

Me: so assface told me about a nude hike. I seriously don't get him.

Max: haha, I seriously don't get you even trying to get him

Me: I think it's just a lifestyle now

Max: well, if I were him, I'd be keeping my options open and you're letting him keep it open, so why would he stop

Me: what should I do?

Max: what you should have been doing this whole time.
   just move on, don't even talk to him, just block him on IM
Me: ughh
Max: just cut him out. I mean, seriously
Me: that's definitely not an option
Max: this is affecting your love life, isn't it? that's not healthy
Me: yes
Max: you're comparing any guy you date with a guy that's
   not even available to you? I mean, insanity really does
   rock your world
Me: sad, I know
Max: I've never heard of anyone cockblocking themselves,
   but you've managed it and it's sad.... you deserve to be
   happy, like truly happy, and I don't think you've been
   for quite some time

So the lesson learned from this conversation was that it's Lily's fault that she's so desirable. Lily *always* has options but somehow is an excellent cockblocker and won't accept any offers no matter how appealing they are. Sounds like the makings of an intriguing biography.

Saturday, August 14, 2010

I should be thrilled that I had so many suitors, yet all I could think each night was, *I'd rather be sleeping* and *he's not Carter*.

The highlight of my week was what I saw on my computer screen when I woke up this morning. The instant I saw my Gmail tab blinking with a notification that I had a message from Carter Swinton, I heard bells ringing and fireworks bursting. The brilliant red, blue, and green sparks momentarily clouded my vision as I felt like celebrating. Right there on my computer screen were a few simple words that made me grin from ear to ear.

2:34 AM Carter: go to sleep

There's no need for him to message me. I never randomly message people to tell them to go to sleep. He's just keeping his contact line with me open and that's just fine with me.

Today, my mommy hosted a fashion party for a few of her girlfriends. Today also happened to be another date night for me. To make my mommy happy, I joined her and her friends for a bit before I had to excuse myself later on to get ready. Thank goodness I met him at his house instead of having him pick me up. I thanked God for that tiny blessing.

I couldn't imagine having all these ladies scrutinize my date and getting involved in my dating life. It was already bad enough with all the questioning I was getting when I said I had to prepare for my date. Once I was all dressed up, I wanted to avoid the guests at all costs.

Right about now, I wished we had a fire escape so I could leave the house unnoticed. But no, I had to walk down the stairs, right through the festivities. And of course I was stopped. Suddenly I had twelve mothers. "Wow! You're beautiful! You're so skinny! There's no way he can't be into you! Look at that sexy shirt! Be good! Don't do anything wrong!" I was barraged with a stream of exclamatory comments. Finally, I managed to find my way to the door, but I could still hear murmurs of the ladies discussing my date, probably living vicariously through me.

In the midst of my urgency to break away from the gossiping ladies and my relief of getting out of the house mildly scathed by my mom and her friends' comments, I did something so bad. Accident or not, it was not good.

Last night, Jeff (the one who wants to marry me) told me the ball was in my court, that I would have to make the next move. I wasn't planning on contacting him anytime soon.

I'm usually very careful about who I send texts and emails to. I mean, I double-check that I'm sending it to the right person. I've seen it happen many times where the message is sent to the wrong recipient and embarrassment is plastered all over the sender.

One particular instance happened at work, where a girl was e-mailing her boyfriend very racy comments and somehow accidentally e-mailed the entire company. I thought I had learned to be absolutely careful.

Today, of all days, I wasn't careful. I was supposed to pick up a few things from my friend Kaleb's house, so I asked, "When can I come over?"

Usually, he takes forever to respond, but I got a reply no sooner than I put my phone down. *That's strange,* I thought. Then I looked at my phone, and then looked at it again, and then did a triple take. Text from Jeff? Why? OMG! I texted him the comment instead of Kaleb. Jeff's response was so eager. "Anytime." Of all the things to text and all the people to text. It was just so perfectly wrong. Poor guy. I really didn't mean to. That was cruel. How could I mix that up? It wasn't even the same name!

I finally got to Reed's house. (He's the neighbor from Facebook. I'll keep reminding you since there are too many guys to keep straight. I can't even keep them straight. I sometimes almost call them the wrong names). He made me a delicious dinner and we just had a chill night. It was a perfect evening, at least it would have been to any normal girl.

Of course, I had to find some flaw. Earlier in the evening, I saw his toenails. They weren't trimmed just right. One or two of his toenails were a little long. They were clean, just not to my liking. That's all I could think about all night. I didn't like his toenails even though that is such an easy fix. I always have to find or create a problem.

I felt like Jerry Seinfeld on his show when he dated a girl who was perfect in every way except for the fact that she had man hands. He couldn't get over that fact and dumped her solely because of her hands. I'm being so nitpicky to the point that, in my mind, only Carter will suffice.

I can never find something wrong with Carter. Just once, I need Carter not to be too good to be true. I needed to find one imperfection, one flaw, one *anything,* that I couldn't discount. I needed to find a reason to give Carter up, if I wanted any chance at a wholesome realationship with someone truly worth my time. Ha, I misspelled relationship, but I like it better that way. *Real*ationship.

Reed's conversation with me was dwindling, so I brought up "my friend's" car, a white Subaru Impreza (Carter's car and Reed is into racing). I always manage to slyly incorporate Carter into conversations. I just like talking about him. What can I say? He's my passion.

The evening ended with a kiss and Reed asking me to spend the night. Oh, there's another guy to add under my belt. I don't even have to be mentally engaged during the date, and I get followers.

Sunday, August 15, 2010

I never get a break from admirers. Trust me, I'm not complaining. I do realize how lucky I am. It's just that it's tiring. My own friend, Colleen, doesn't even like talking to me sometimes and has to take a break from me because she's so envious of all the attention I get. This fact just reaffirms why most of my friends are guys and why every chick I meet immediately dislikes me for fear of competition. I'm often seen as a threat.

The funny thing is that I'm completely harmless. I would never hurt a fly, and I would never be a home wrecker, at least not intentionally. It has been known to happen on occasion, but not by any doing of my own. I was an innocent bystander who got sucked into the drama. I'm not drama at all, but somehow drama follows me everywhere.

❧⁓❧

I went to my friend Noah's house. (I met him in Greece three years ago. He professed his love for me then). Sometimes, against my better judgment, I want the friendship from these guys; they're just so cool. But, I know better. I should never ignore my gut feelings.

The plan was to go swimming in his pool. It was definitely a hot day, but when the first thing that came out of his mouth was, "Let's get in the water, let me see you in that bikini, which you look great in but don't wear often enough," I decided not to take my dress off. I really wanted to go swimming too, but I wasn't in the mood to be looked at like a piece of meat today. I've already been getting that all week.

All day he made comments like, "Lily, just give me a chance. I want to take care of you, and I'd take great care of you. Let me be your man. I'm a patient man. I know it will happen one day." Oh, give it a rest. It's been three years already, and I haven't shown *any* interest.

Oh wait, is that what I sound like about Carter? That's pathetic. I've been waiting around for *ten* years. Okay, but let me rationalize here. Carter has shown an interest in me. Everyone knows he's interested in me, maybe not to the same extent I am, but there is some inkling of desire on his end.

However, I've *never* alluded to the fact that I want something more from Noah, so you see, this is a *very* different situation.

Noah made the day all about me and asked me where I wanted to go eat. I suggested California Vegan in Santa Monica. That was me including Carter. Just the other day, Carter posted up a picture of this restaurant, California Vegan, in Santa Monica, on his Facebook and raved about the food. I wanted to go because he went, not necessarily for the amazing food. I just wanted to have the chance to sit where he might have been sitting.

I like to live in his footsteps. Whatever he does, I do afterward. Maybe it's me trying too hard to make us have similar interests. Maybe it's just great timing. I always find that the situations naturally fall into my lap. I would never go out of my way to go where Carter went. For some reason, I happened to be nearby this restaurant shortly after he posted the picture.

Noah had a very hard time saying good-bye to me. I, on the other hand, had no problem leaving. I don't want anyone badly enough, and that's why they want me so badly.

My friend calls this the classic forbidden apple situation. Adam and Eve never wanted a fruit as badly as the one they weren't supposed to have. They had their choice of any and every fruit, but they wanted the one untouchable fruit, the one that would lead to their demise.

The more elusive I am, the more appealing I become, which equates to a challenge, which means I'm the perfect girl every time.

Monday, August 16, 2010

I didn't think I could have a more jam-packed week of boys than last week, but in the life of Lily, always expect the unexpected. (I should just make the unexpected the expected).

I got five phone calls today, all from male friends. Not a single girl contacted me today. No wonder every chick hates me. Every one of their guys loves me.

One of the most memorable phone calls was from Eric (Carter's cousin). He specifically called to remind me not to talk about church camp at the Rodrigo y Gabriela concert we were going to attend on Wednesday together. He's bringing his girlfriend, Sara (I'm pretty sure she doesn't like me very much), and I'm bringing Rico (the ex-boyfriend who is still in love with me).

Upon asking why I can't talk about church camp in front of her, Eric said, "Because I told her that I had no reception up there (mountains of San Bernardino) so I wouldn't have to call her, but

I called you three times. She can't know that I talked to you and not to her."

"Oh," I said. "That's fine." (This kind of crap happens to me all the time. I'm a secret and always have to keep secrets). "As long as you don't talk about Carter." (Rico despises Carter because he was an issue during our relationship). We both started laughing. It's almost like we were having an affair or a secret relationship, except nothing ever happened or ever will happen.

Eric and I definitely have some cool connection, just not romantic, even though he thinks so. So basically, we can only talk about the future, no bringing up the past when we see each other. Too funny.

I went to my best friend Anna's house tonight just to chill. Of course, we indulged in my favorite activity—looking at Carter's Facebook page—and checked out some of his pictures with Brook, the blonde bimbo.

We started making fun of her, then took our fun to the next level and said, "Why are you pulling a Brook? Don't be like Brook. Only Brook would do that. There's nothing to her except that she looks like Barbie." Poor girl. We were sabotaging her. Oh well, it was fun, and it made me feel better.

From the pictures on his Facebook, Anna and I decided that Brook just fed his ego. She had a classic conventional beauty to her, the kind that you see in magazines (not my type at all). That's exactly it; it's flat and two dimensional and boring, just like she is in all her Facebook pictures. She looked so lifeless and void of a personality. Anna and I were convinced that Brook was a novelty that would wear off, for sure.

Brook, you're boring. Sorry, girlfriend, move over for the real goods. You may be the original ditzy Barbie, but times have changed. Carter wants the exotic Egyptian Barbie with brains.

Your looks can't get you by forever, bimbo. Your time will pass, and then *my* time will come.

Later that night, I told my sister all my thoughts, and I figured she would laugh. Quite the contrary, she looked at me with sad eyes. "Do you really feel like the misery you're living through the first half of your life will be worth the happiness that you *think* you will get from him during the second half of your life, *if* he even decides that you're the one? Will the second half of your life, if you spend it with him, make up for this miserable part? Will it be fulfilling enough for what you've gone through?" my sister asked. She's so profound sometimes.

My answer, as I'm sure you all know, was, "Yes, without a doubt." I'm narrating my own sob story, and I see how pathetic I look, but I can't help but feel we are destined to be together. A dream you don't fight for can haunt you for the rest of your life. Someday our universes will collide, and we will be one.

Tuesday, August 17, 2010

My high school students took such an interest in my life, especially my dating life. It's no wonder that Carter constantly came up in conversation. It never failed to amaze me how excited I got simply to mention him.

Before leaving for lunch, I glanced at my Gchat. Because Assface was fresh on my mind with all the questions my students asked, I misinterpreted Anna's instant message to me about her friend: "Tammy is dating an assface."

What! I was furious. My heart started racing, and I was about ready to punch something. Then I read it again and calmed down. I read it too fast. I thought it said that Tammy was dating Assface (sans *an*). That tiny word made a big difference. It wouldn't even make sense that Tammy is dating him because Carter is dating bimbo girl. Ay, Lily.

I get so irrational so quickly when it comes to Assface. It's almost as if I coined the term "assface" and that it can only be used to describe Carter Swinton. That word in any other context doesn't even exist to my brain. The sole purpose of that word is strictly for Carter.

On the way home from work, I was listening to a Christian radio station and heard something interesting. "Once you broadcast your sins, then you can cling to Jesus, and healing can begin." Carter is my biggest sin. I think about him *all* the time, 24/7. If my job were to think about Carter Swinton, I would be a millionaire, no, a billionaire. I would get overtime all the time. I would have job security for life. It would be a very lucrative career.

He's my sin because I think about him more than I think about God. It's almost as if Carter is my God. I've placed him on a towering pedestal, and I don't know how to bring him down. I keep lifting him higher and higher.

I get that he's flawed and has faults just like every other human being, but I just don't have eyes for them. I turn a blind eye to anything negative with Carter. It's true, lust glosses over off-putting qualities. I don't even know if I want to heal. I've gotten so used to this miserable life of fantasy that it's almost bearable, and even enjoyable, now.

Wednesday, August 18, 2010

Carter changed his status on Gchat. Today it said, "Thurs@hot. springs." Does that mean he's going to the hot springs again with Brook? *Ughh! Save some activities for me, Carter. I want to do fun things with you. Don't waste them all on her!*

Tonight was the night of the Rodrigo y Gabriela concert with Eric, his girlfriend, Sara, and my ex-boyfriend, Rico. Apart from the interesting dynamics between the four of us, the night was amazing and made up for the crap I realized today (hot spring outings without me).

Eric was giving me more attention than he was giving to Sara, and I could feel the waves of jealousy. It didn't help that Rico was treating me like a queen all night. He was massaging me the entire night. True to our word, I didn't talk about church camp, and Eric didn't talk about Carter. Phew (wiping sweat off my brow)!

Jealousy seemed to be the theme of the night. Just in the car on the way to the concert, Rico made a point of saying he didn't like to get involved with my Facebook. He detested looking at it because everyone loves me. His exact words were, "Everyone loves you. Every time I look at your Facebook, I see something I don't like and get jealous, so I just decided not to look at it at all. I'm the only one who can love you."

Here we go again. He thinks we're dating again. He probably thought tonight was a serious double date. Can you imagine what he would say if he heard Eric say anything about Carter, if he's already jealous of insignificant people on my Facebook?

Rico loathed Carter for many reasons. The biggest reason was that I came into the relationship with Rico with Assface baggage and told him about it on our first date. He noticed my angst and mentioned that it was a red flag but was willing to deal with the repercussions, hoping he could "cure" me of the infamous Assface. Apparently, my Carter issues never went away, thus the animosity from Rico toward Carter.

Thursday, August 19, 2010

I changed my Gchat status to "Best concert ever!" and posted a link to my favorite song by Rodrigo y Gabriela. No sooner had I changed my status than Carter instant messaged me. I literally posted the link, turned away from the computer for a brief moment, looked back, and saw the blinking orange box in my Gchat from Carter.

> Carter: dudeee...I was trying to find people to go with me
>   to them at the greeeeek. so good huh?
> Me: yes!
> Carter: very cool. listening to their pandora station when
>   I saw ur status

Okay, so it's obvious he checks out my status messages. He's checking me out any way he can. This is why I comment and write on so many boys' pages on Facebook. I'm being sneaky. If he looks at my Facebook page and sees how many guys I talk to on a regular basis, he might get jealous and start wondering why he's not included in my circle of love.

It's true, everyone loves me. Not everyone loves Brook, though. She's supposed to be a well-known model, and her "hot" bikini picture only has seven comments, while my profile picture has seventeen comments. I'm not even famous.

I'm so calculated. It makes my head hurt, but I gotta do what I gotta do to get this guy.

I was on the phone with Eric when Carter messaged me. I told Eric, and he said, "Don't worry about Carter. He'll be back for you as soon as he gets tired of his blonde bimbo."

Then I asked, "If Carter cares so much about me, then why isn't he with me?"

"Because he feels trapped with you, Lily. Otherwise, he would be with you." That's funny. I didn't like that comment. Most guys I date tell me that I'm too chill. But then Eric redeemed himself with his next comment. "He'll come back to you when he's ready to be trapped."

Interesting concept, Eric, but I guess it makes sense. Anything that mentions Carter coming back to me, I'll take.

Friday, August 20, 2010

I had a voice lesson today with Nora, the psychic. I brought her a picture of Carter so she could have a visual. She thought he was hot just like everyone else. It can't be denied; he's smokin' hot. After looking at the picture, she said, "I'll see what I can do to help you out." Uhm, what does that even mean? She isn't God, but I do sincerely appreciate the notion of her trying to speed up fate.

I went to Reed's house tonight, and we talked about how he drinks a lot and how I drink not at all. I asked him if he was okay hanging out with a nonalcoholic, and he said it was okay as long as I was willing to hang out with an alcoholic. See, it can be done.

Carter gave me the excuse that drinking is a part of his lifestyle and that it would be difficult to hang out since I don't partake in that activity. I guess if you like someone enough, you'll be okay with whatever and however they are. Stupid Carter.

After my date with Reed, I felt the need to talk about Carter. It's as if every guy I date fuels the Carter fire. I just want him more. So I called Holly, a friend from my sorority, and was complaining about the blonde bimbo girlfriend. I whined, "He can't have everything. He can't have her and talk to me on the side."

Holly agreed, "No, he can't have everything, and you are everything. You need a guy who knows that you are everything." She continued, "Lily, you really are smart most of the time, but not with Carter. You really are a dumb bunny when it comes to Assface." Leave it to her to be utterly honest. I love her. She tells it like it is.

She's right, "I am everything." He needs to take my everything rather than try and pick pieces of me. It's all or nothing, AF.

Saturday, August 21, 2010

I ran a mud run with my friend Preston this morning. Last time I saw him was in April. Last time I saw him, I told him about my three months of counseling sessions and that it was one of the most beneficial things I did for myself. I learned a lot about myself and how to deal with many issues in my life.

This time, Preston told me that he went to eight counseling sessions because of me. "Lily, you are perfect and there is nothing wrong with you. You are too cool, and everything you do is inspiring. If you say you enjoyed something, I'll try it." I'm honored that he thinks so highly of me and my lifestyle.

I impact so many people's lives. God, you are using me to reach out to people to make them feel better about themselves. That is my gift: giving people better self-esteem and confidence. When will I be able to use my gift with Carter? He doesn't seem to be phased by my goodness at all.

Preston said that when the counselor asked him why he came, he said that he was there because "my friend Lily went to a counselor and thought it was a good experience, and she's really cool, so I'm doing it too." I can't get over the fact that I truly inspired him to go to eight sessions.

I live my life off the beaten path, and I think that's what is truly inspiring to others. I go against the grain. I do what I want to do. I do what other people want to do but don't have the guts to put into action. Thank you, God, for working through me.

Tonight I went to a party and met a girl who started openly talking about her relationship. I was really trying to make it a point not to bring up Carter since most people at this party don't know anything about me. But she insisted on asking about my past relationships and, whoops, Assface slipped out. Of course, she was interested in why I was so ridiculously stuck on Assface. She asked me to give five reasons why I like him:

1. He has goals and aspirations and actually tries to achieve them.
2. He makes me laugh.
3. We have the same interests, outdoor activities.

4. He has a stable and steady job.
5. We come from the same religious background. (It means nothing now, it's our biggest fundamental difference.)

She was impressed that I didn't mention any of his physical traits on the list. To be honest, I was impressed with myself also. I usually start off with the fact that he's hot. That he looks just like the actor, Josh Lucas or Bradley Cooper. I wonder if he's ever made a list about me.

Sunday, August 22, 2010

Today's church message was excellent. It pertained well to my life. In order to hear God, you need to practice listening. In order for God to work through you, He needs you. We can't do without Him, but He can do without us. We need to let Him in to give us the strength to get through life. We should be amazed at what happens in our life through God's help.

Faith is a deliberate confidence in the character of God whose ways you may not understand at the time. Having faith means trusting in advance what will only make sense in reverse. If we take a backseat to our lives and let God take the steering wheel, by His Grace, He will empower us and work through us to do immeasurably more. His will will be done, and His kingdom will come.

The problem with people today is that God has a dream for each and every one of us, but we try to make *our* dreams a reality. There is too much temptation to do everything in our own strength. God made some of us too talented for our own good. No matter what, we need to let God's dream for us guide our life, and we will be eternally happier. Everyone's motto should be, "Hey God, whatever You want to do, whenever You want to do it, I trust You."

You have no idea how difficult this concept is for me. The last ten years of my life, I've been trying to make Carter date me. I go to events and do things with thoughts of Carter in the back of my mind. I'm a planner; I always have an ulterior motive. *Will Carter like this? Would Carter do this? What would Carter say in this situation?*

I hate that I let Carter have a hold on me. I hate that Carter consumes my every thought and every move. I hate that Carter's actions determine my mood. I hate that Carter has no idea how much I care. I hate that I can't get over him.

I clearly need to take today's sermon to heart. I'm not God. I should let God be God and I should just be Lily.

On Facebook today, Ron, a guy I haven't talked to in literally years, messaged me. We got to talking, and of course, it came up that, "Lily, you're amazing. I always liked you." The whole "out of sight, out of mind" concept doesn't exist with anything or anyone who has to do with me. Everyone comes back for more.

It seems that I season with age. The longer anyone is away from me, the more they find me attractive as a whole. I do lead a very interesting life. I wonder if Carter would ever consider me amazing.

This concept of being amazing doesn't just stop with men. Whenever I try on shoes, no matter where I am, someone *always* comments on how I look in the shoes. Sometimes they even pick out shoes for me to try on. When I asked my sister if that happened to her, she said it *never* happened to her. Wow. It literally happens *every* time, and I go shoe shopping a lot.

Just today, I went to three different stores and had multiple women comment in each store. There is definitely something about me. I'm just that approachable. My karma is good. My aura is good. Maybe it's just that people see the light of God in me and don't realize what they are looking at but know that I'm safe.

Again, thank you, God. You are my life. You've made my life. All that I have is because of You. Please let me honor You.

Monday, August 23, 2010

My best friend, Anna, has been out of town for a week. When she's in town, we talk daily, and sometimes even multiple times a day. She's my makeshift boyfriend. You'd think that I'd miss her when she leaves the country, and I do, but I don't mind that the Pause button is held down. I have no problem holding that Pause button down and being able to pick up right where we left off.

However, there is no Pause button with Carter. I've even tried to force it down, but it's as if the button is broken. Carter Swinton in Lily's mind doesn't pause. There is no such thing. A week away from a friend flies by, yet a week away from Carter is an eternity. Funny how that works.

Tuesday, August 24, 2010

When I miss Carter, which is all the time, I sometimes call Rico just to satisfy my craving for attention. But after watching the movie, *Eat, Pray, Love,* and hearing a wise man tell a woman with a broken heart how to be strong, I decided to take a different approach to Carter.

Let me lay down some ground rules for myself. I can miss him. I can send him love every time I think about him, rather than anger. I need to clear out all the space in my mind that I'm using to obsess over Carter in order to create a doorway. God will rush in and fill me with more love than I've ever dreamed. Okay, Lily, time for a backbone rather than a wishbone.

I'm going to wish him well every time I think of him. Over time, I'm sure my positive thoughts will overtake any bitterness and anger I hold, and I will have created an empty vessel for God to fill, as my mom once advised me to do.

Wednesday, August 25, 2010

I woke up today a changed woman. I came to the realization that Carter cares very deeply for me, but it's just that. Sometimes you can love someone with all your heart and soul, but only from a distance. I have to be satisfied with that. I'm at peace with Carter. I don't need to be chasing him or be bitter that he's dating someone else. There's no point in that. That's the way life goes. Maybe he'll come to realize how much better I am than the girl he is dating—and maybe not.

God always has a plan. I am certain of it, and I trust it wholeheartedly.

Thursday, August 26, 2010

In class today, I was using variables (letters) to explain a geometry topic. I picked *L* and *C*. Instead of leaving it at that, I of course had to explain why I chose those letters. I said, "*L* for *Lily* and *C* for the name of the guy I have a crush on."

My students laughed, but really, that's pathetic. As my students were working independently and I was roaming the room, I could hear the music from one of the iPods. It was "Bulletproof," by La Roux. I interrupted my student to tell her I love that song, and she confidently said, "It's your new favorite song because of your ex, huh?" These kids don't let anything get past them. This was Yelena, the student who counseled me weeks earlier. I like her. After class, Maggie, another teacher, came into my classroom and started discussing Carter and all the recent dates I've been on. I explained to her my feelings again, which are always the same—I am not interested in anyone I'm dating. I'm still holding out for Carter. (She asks me on a weekly basis; she's like my second mother).

She emphatically noted, "Fate can't be changed. You just know deep down. (This in reference to my extreme, strong notion that

171

Carter and I will end up together). There is a Chinese proverb that says that whatever is yours will not be taken away from you."

"But, Lily," she continued with all seriousness, "fight for what you want, but take a break. Even wars have breaks."

I liked that comment. I could work with that.

Friday, August 27, 2010

I woke up in a gooood mood. So good that on casual Friday at work, I wore a skirt and heels, and did my hair. Everyone thought that I was dressed nicely for a hot date after work. Nah. I just felt good about not obsessing over Carter for the last few days. It felt nice to be at peace with the situation.

It didn't mean that I didn't think about him at all, because I still did, a lot. During our in-service at work today, I kept daydreaming about what kind of gifts Carter would give me, if we were together. When the presenter suddenly glared at me, I realized I had chuckled just a little too loudly at a very inappropriate time, as he discussed upcoming layoffs in the company.

But, I couldn't keep it together when the thought popped into my mind that Carter would send me a basket full of tomatoes, bell peppers, and onions over a basket full of flowers.

Every occasion he could, Carter would remind me that I was missing out on the best tastes in the world. He'd get a kick out of offering me some of his food, which was always seasoned with tomatoes, bell peppers, or onions, knowing that I'd shudder while simultaneously making the face of disappointment. He loved my reaction. He loved me. I know he did. I just don't know what happened to make him back off.

A basket full of the three vegetables I have no desire to ever put in my mouth would not only be funny, but it would also show that the guy listens to what I say and knows something about me. That shows character. Not any guy would have the guts to send a gift like that. I know that Carter would, and that's why I like him as much as I do. He would do silly stuff like that. I like silly.

Saturday, August 28, 2010

Summiting San Gorgonio Peak via Vivian Creek in the San Bernardino Mountains was an amazing experience. Two friends and I hiked 19 miles with a 6,000-foot elevation gain in one day. It took us ten hours. This hike was my idea, which originated from Carter. He recommended this hike to me as practice for Mt. Whitney.

The entire time I was hiking, I was thinking about Carter, rather than living in the present and enjoying my friends' company. All I could think about was how Carter walked this same path. I thought about how we were living parallel lives. We did the same activities, but never together. We suggested activities for each other and got excited when we explained them to each other, but for some reason, we have never had a chance to enjoy them together.

I'm too afraid to ask him, for fear of rejection; and he probably doesn't want to ask me because he doesn't want me to think that we are in a relationship when in fact, we should be in a relationship. We enjoy too many of the same activities. We're perfect for each other.

Just the other day, he mentioned that he couldn't find anyone to go with him to the Rodrigo y Gabriela concert, which I went to. How ironic that he didn't go. It just gives me more ammunition to believe that we are meant to be together. In due time, he will realize that.

After the intense hike, I went to my friend Jace's birthday party. I was exhausted and, I'm sure, did not look my best. But for some reason, that's when men find me most attractive. That night I met Ben Ents, Jace's friend, and could immediately tell he was very interested. I was wiped out from the day, so I only stayed for about forty-five minutes.

On my way out, he mentioned a 5K run that he would be doing in a few weeks and asked me if I would be interested in participating. He got my number. I was so tired I didn't even put two and two together. He just used the 5K run as a line.

Sunday, August 29, 2010

Parker, the guy I went on a date with to the Art Walk, called today with exciting news, for him. He said he bought two VIP tickets to a jazz festival for us. I couldn't have been less excited. He never even asked if I could go or not.

I used my family as an excuse; I didn't want to go with him anyway. I needed to find a way to get rid of him. He was disappointed when I told him I wouldn't be able to make it, like I was obliged to accompany him. As if that wasn't enough, Ben from last night, called, wanting to take me out on a dinner date. I didn't go.

I'm too nice. I say yes to go out with these boys then can't get rid of them. Usually, saying yes to go on a date is a sign that there is some sort of interest. I, however, say yes just to say yes; that way no one can accuse me of not putting myself out there and holding out for Carter.

I end up getting stuck with boys who fall in love with me immediately. I'm telling you, the more I don't like them, the more they want me. I don't get it.

Unfortunately, I don't learn my lesson. I seem to be an expert on running into brick walls, backing up, and running into them faster, rather than climbing over them.

Today, I had an argument with my mom. That's no surprise. We argue every time we talk. It's been said that the parent you argue with the most is the one you are most similar to. It's true. I am my mother's daughter; the apple doesn't fall far from the tree. What I need to learn with her is to manage my point-blank demeanor. It gets me all my admirers, but doesn't get me very far with my mom.

The one person who can calm me down after an argument with my mom is Rico, the UFC ex. He's truly a Lily whisperer. It's quite unfortunate that we aren't right for each other. He said that being point-blank means that I am more intelligent than I need to be.

He told me to slow my roll in life and be more empathetic to people's needs, especially my mom's. In the same breath, he also said that there are very few people who have a zest for life as intense as I do. He said that I understand that time is ticking and I try to fill it with as many activities as possible.

Most people, he mentioned, can't keep up with that and either get agitated with me or become jealous of me. That absolutely makes sense, Rico! My mom and I bicker daily because she thinks I do too much and don't pay enough attention to family. Rico, you are so smart. I know I keep you around for something.

I've always thought it was strange that I have a hard time hearing lower-pitched, rough, rumbly voices like Assface's. Every time Carter and I would talk, I would have to ask him to repeat himself, not because he mumbled, but one, because his voice hypnotized me- I could listen to him read the yellow pages all day; two, I had difficulty making out his words.

I told my sister about this right before she did a hearing test on me with an audiometer she brought home from school. (She's studying to become a speech therapist). The results showed that I have excellent hearing *except* for some of the lower-pitched tones. She was amazed that I knew this about myself. I don't mind struggling to hear what Carter says. I just want to be with him. Someday, not hearing him well could be an advantage.

Someone's Facebook status said, "If you love someone, set them free. If you have to stalk them, it's not meant to be."

I thought that was clever. It's clever enough that I may give up looking at Assface's Facebook for the *entire* month of September. As of now, I still have a few days to check out his page.

Monday, August 30, 2010

Ben called today to hang out since I couldn't hang out yesterday. Thank goodness I couldn't go because I had to work until 10:00 p.m. So he asked, "What will it take to go out with Mademoiselle Lily? I want to see you." He continually complimented me, and while most guys got annoyed that I work until 10:00 p.m. tutoring, he turned it around and said that he really admired my civic-mindedness, my attention to helping others. Ugh! Can I really do no wrong? *Where is Carter? Why doesn't he think this about me?*

Tuesday, August 31, 2010

I love waking up to dreams about Carter. This one was quite simple, yet it still made me smile. I have a picture of Carter and myself that I put on my nightstand facing me. It's the first and last thing I see every morning and night. I'm trying to create Carter dreams. Even if it isn't as effective as I would like it to be, I just like looking at him.

The dream was simply that Carter called on a Thursday to ask me what I was doing on Friday because he wanted to talk to me with his friend on the phone. He wanted to talk seriously and wanted someone to witness it, and then he wanted to see me. Simple, yet effective.

Today was my last day to stalk Carter on Facebook. Then I have to be celibate for thirty days. I can do it. I gave up sweets and bread for thirty-one days, during a holiday month.

I got a text from a guy who is twice my age and is in love with me. "Can I fly you to Missouri for Labor Day weekend to be my date at my class reunion?"

Every day is something new. Every day I have to come up with excuses not to be able to hang out. I don't want to fight boys off anymore. I want Carter to chase after me as desperately as these other guys have been chasing after me, year in and year out. Have I been running after someone who's already gone?

Wednesday, September 1, 2010

I had the day off today to go to my uncle's funeral. Don't worry. Everyone was fine. It's better this way. He is in heaven. The positive side to this is that I had a chance to sit down with an Orthodox priest and ask some questions I had about my faith.

Although, I have no qualms with my faith, I was asking with an ulterior motive, for Carter. I want so badly to be able to explain to Carter why it is that I believe wholeheartedly in Orthodoxy. I don't want to be stumped when asked questions about my religion. I want to be able to explain the phenomena of my religion to people who don't necessarily believe (i.e., Carter).

He has so many reasons why he doesn't believe. I just want to be able to rebut. I asked the question that most nonbelievers have a hard time wrapping their head around: "How can the wine and bread for communion be converted into the true body and blood of Christ?"

First of all, most Orthodox Christians don't even believe this concept, so how do you explain it to a nonbeliever? I was awed by the answer I received. It definitely gave me a better grasp on the concept. "There are many things in the Orthodox faith that are a mystery. You just have to believe and have faith.

For example, let's say you live in a room with no windows or doors; it would be very dark. Now let's say you modify the room and give it a very small circular window. Now you can see a few rays of light, feel the warmth of the sun, and see the blue skies and the lush outdoor scenery; the beauty of it all boggles your mind. This room with the little window is you, a human being with your limitations.

Now, with what little you can see and feel from the tiny window, you can assume with certainty that the sun, sky, and nature exist on a much larger scale. This is how religion works. You cannot see everything you desire to see; you just must believe it. This is what faith is.

Much of religion is a mystery like the seven sacraments. When you are Chrismated (anointed after baptism), the priest talks about your new nature, which cannot be seen, just believed. In the sacrament of marriage, two become one, but you cannot see this phenomenon. The man and the woman do not merge into one; it is just believed as so.

Similarly, communion is about eating the body and blood of Christ. You can't see it turn into flesh and blood, but you believe that it is so. This is faith. It's not believing blindly; it's believing in the miracles of God. You cannot see God, but that doesn't mean that He doesn't exist. We are but miniscule beings who cannot fathom the greatness of God with our eyes, so we must rely on our beliefs."

That was an excellent answer. I hope Carter asks me so that I can explain it to him, and he can be impressed.

That was the morning. This evening, I went to the Hollywood Bowl with Rico to go see a concert. I would have much rather gone with Carter, but I had to work with what was given to me. Or is that cruel?

Rico was talking about a girl he met today and their conversation. He quickly said, "I mean, I didn't meet her. She was a customer at the store. I don't want to meet girls." Oh Rico, I want you to meet girls, but that won't happen because you love me too much and are willing to be miserable with me.

Thursday, September 2, 2010

I gave in. I went out on a date with Ben today. We went to a little café, which I loved more than the time spent with him. Within the first fifteen minutes of hanging out, he guessed my Myers-Briggs personality letters perfectly and gave me reasons for why I was each letter (Introverted iNtuitive Feeling Judging). He was on a roll, so he thought. He couldn't contain holding in his secret any longer and nearly burst a vein explaining his self-proclaimed cleverness. Ben confessed that the 5K run he told me about was a hoax; he was so proud that it worked. I just stared at him.

He never signed up for a run and was never planning on it. He just needed a way to get my number without sounding creepy. I was so done with tonight. By the end of the short night, because I was exhausted and because his confession completely turned me off, he said he really, really liked me and was willing to not move to England for his new job to be with me.

What is it with you, boys? What did I do? All I do is talk about myself and ask a few get-to-know-you questions. I even talked about this journal that I'm writing about Carter, and he was still interested. Guys come out of the woodwork for me. I'm either every guy's best friend, you know, one of the guys, or I'm every guy's addiction.

Eventually, down the road, they *all* realize that Lily is a girl too, end up falling in love, and professing their undying love for me, as if the world were going to end tomorrow.

They all come out at the same time is what it feels like, but the truth is that I just have a constant, steady stream of guys always after me. I don't get any breaks. Again, I'm not complaining, but I just wish it were Assfart, as my friend Ray calls him.

It's so nice when people acknowledge your beauty online, on a public domain like Facebook. I don't need constant praise or compliments, but I do like getting them where Carter can see that I'm admired. So when Janet posted this on my wall, I got excited.

"OMG I know you're gorgeous, but the profile pic is amazing!"

Thanks, Janet! You rock! The other thing about Facebook is that just today, on three different occasions, it suggested that I reach out and say hello to Carter Swinton. It's never made that suggestion to me before. Whatever. I may be reading into this one too much because Facebook is totally random anyway. Oh well, that's the story of my life.

Friday, September 3, 2010

I'm such a heartbreaker, totally not on purpose. I was trying to call a student I tutor, Justin Darvis, to let him know that I was running late, but I would be there shortly. I didn't pay attention when I selected the number on my cell phone. Instead of calling Justin Darvis, I called another, Justin—a guy I met through online dating—who fell in love with me on the first date and professed his love for me just like every other guy.

Over the years, he still would drop me texts saying he missed me. I never responded. As soon as he answered, I said, "Hey Justin, I'm sorry I'm late. I'm supposed to be at your house at 7:15, but I got stuck in traffic. I should be there no later than 7:30."

Justin's response: "You're coming over? Right now?"

Not realizing my mistake, with irritation I responded, "Yes, I come over every Tuesday and Thursday night at 7:15. That's our routine."

Again, he asked with bafflement, "You're coming over right now?"

What is wrong with this kid? I always go tutor him, and he's so responsible. Then I looked at my phone and finally noticed that I called the *wrong* Justin. I quickly said, "Sorry, I have the wrong number," as if that would fix the wound I know I opened. And without giving him a chance to say anything, I hung up.

No wonder he sounded genuinely excited and eager to see me. I'm losing it these days. I have too much on my plate, and I'm not paying attention to details. I keep calling or texting some sensitive people. This is bad karma even though I'm not doing it on purpose.

God help me get my head on straight and relax. I do need to slow my roll, as Rico so frequently said to me. I want to create genuine happiness, not misery.

What's my problem? Let me try to sort through my thoughts. In my eyes, Carter is too good to be true. I think Carter is perfect and I put him on a pedestal. I think *I'm* not good enough for Carter. Maybe I'm not good enough for me. I had an *aha* moment.

I do put Carter on a pedestal, and I do think he's God's gift to women. I, by no means, have a low self-esteem. But when it comes to Carter, I think he's better than me. My issue is clearly that *I* don't think I'm good enough for him. The truth is I'm more than ideal for Assface. I'm probably too good for him.

Saturday, September 4, 2010

Eric, Carter's cousin, called me today inviting me to go to a Greek festival with him next week. However, it all had to be done in secret. We couldn't get there right at the same time, and when we did "run" into each other, we had to pretend like it was a coincidence that we were both at the festival.

We had to take all these precautions because of his jealous-ass girlfriend, Sara. What's even worse, Eric was calling me from the grocery store and setting a twenty-minute limit on our phone call because he was sent by Sara to run an errand that wouldn't take more than twenty minutes. It's seriously like I'm having an affair with Eric. I don't even like the guy in that way. I can never be best buddies with Sara.

After Eric called, my mommy called. I told her about my date with Ben and how uninterested I was. I'm glad he's moving to England soon so that I don't have to find an excuse not to talk to him. She just flatly said, "May God bring Carter to you since you don't like anyone else."

Ha. I guess there's nothing more to say. I have a one-track mind.

Sunday, September 5, 2010

Do you know what it's like getting up every morning feeling hopeless because the love of your life is waking up next to the wrong girl? Yet, at the same time, hoping that he finds happiness, even if it's never going to be with you?

I want all the best for Carter, and I want that life of his to be shared with me, but if I can't be with him, I do want him to live a happy life.

I remember when he first told me about this new girl, before I knew anything about her. I said, "I hope it works out." He instantly said, "You don't have to say that." The truth is I want him to be happy with or without me, and I want him to know that his happiness makes me happy. I just wish it were with someone I approved of. That's what true love is, always wanting what's best for someone, even if that doesn't include you.

Daydreaming about Carter, as usual, I was thinking if I could guess all of his Myers-Briggs letters. I don't even know if I know him well enough. I think that he is an introverted extrovert (emphasis on the second adjective). I believe he likes being alone (watching movies in bed) sometimes, but he gets his energy from socializing. I stopped there. Why am I even doing this? When will this ever be relevant to my life?

Carter was in Texas this weekend working on a farm and visiting family. I want to visit Texas so badly, and I want to work on a farm just as badly. I wonder if during his trip he ever thought about me. I mean, did he ever think, *Lily would totally enjoy doing this. Or This would be fun to do with Lily.* He can't think that blonde girlie chick would enjoy humidity and farm work. What fun is that to have a girlfriend who's going to sit inside while you bust your butt working?

Today was a day of reflections. Carter hadn't contacted me in a while, but the thought crossed my mind that he *shouldn't* be contacting me at all. The fact that he had been says a lot. Throughout all my relationships, I never cut Carter out of my life. I was always communicating with him. I cut the cord with all the other guys, but not Carter. The reason I never stopped talking to him was because I was never truly serious in any of my relationships. (I didn't know that then, but I know that now).

He's doing the same thing. I can't say for certain that he doesn't talk to other girls, but I know that our brief online chats are underlined with flirting and softness, our own version of trysts. He is still on the hunt for the perfect match, for his soul mate. There is really no reason for him to keep me around, even as a friend.

Soooo, my conclusion is that this chick is not the one for him. It takes time to realize these things. He probably has no idea that he doesn't want to be with her forever; he just knows that I am important enough to keep around.

Monday, September 6, 2010

Ben called today to invite me out on Saturday. I told him persistence didn't work on me. In my mind, I was reaching for anything to get rid of him; but instead, he said, "That's a huge turn-on." I continued talking about myself giving the allusion that I had a big head, and he said with admiration, "I like that you're cool and that you know you're cool."

I just can't win with these guys. I try not to show interest, and I get more interest.

My sister said I'm obsessed with Carter because I think about him 24/7 and with such detail. In my defense, I told her that if I were obsessed after ten years, I would be considered a psycho. "Angie, do you think I'm a psycho?" She pondered what I said for a moment and said no, but she didn't understand why I couldn't get him out of my mind.

I told her I have a one-track mind. When I want something, I go after it until I get it, no ifs, ands, or buts. It's called tenacity. This just happens to be the longest journey I've been on to get what I want. I don't take no for an answer.

I'm already planning what to wear to the Greek festival next week just on the off chance that I might run into him. I even have conversations planned out in case I meet Brook.

Yvonne, my coworker, and I are in love with men that we can't have. She's married and lusts after someone from her past, and Carter has a serious girlfriend, yet we still think we have a chance. I said, "Nothing helps…counseling doesn't help, being married doesn't help, other boys don't help." We are just both messed up in the head. That's probably why we are best friends.

Tuesday, September 7, 2010

I didn't want to go to work today after my wisdom teeth extraction on Friday. I was tired and exhausted and was having a hard time even talking. I was seriously considering taking the day off, but I didn't. Instead, I trudged to work and hoped that I wouldn't have a heavy load of students today.

What do you know? God sent me only two students today! Do you know how unheard of that is? I usually see fifteen to twenty students daily. This gave me a chance to recuperate. I believe wholeheartedly that this was nothing short of a miracle. There is no way that there is no God. Life is just too perfect. The puzzle pieces of life fit perfectly together. No human could have made it more perfect.

Now my qualm is this: I know that God exists, and I know He has a plan for us all, but I can't figure out what my plan is or why Carter even entered my plan. I don't know what lesson I should be learning from him being in my life. I don't want to go against God's will and continue aching for Carter, but I am having a hard time with His purpose.

As I mentioned before, everyone has a purpose in life and in each other's lives. *Is it to teach me a lesson about how I treat the boys in my life? Am I getting the same treatment I give to others? Am I getting punished for torturing boys?*

God, please give me a sign. Please. Or maybe You are giving me signs, and I am still choosing to ignore them. If that's the case, then give me the strength to open my eyes and take the news with grace even if I don't like it. Your plan is greater than any sorrow I may have right now.

Carter wasn't online all day today. He should have been back from Texas already, I thought. It makes me sad when he isn't online. I don't know where he is, and I don't have the option of accessing him. I just like to glance over and see his name on the side of my computer screen. It's comforting to know he's online, that he's just simply there.

It's like parking your car in front of the window of a restaurant and making sure you can see it out of the corner of your eye to make sure that it's still there. It's just comforting knowing that the car is simply there.

My sister and I come across unique people: my ex, Rico, who thinks he can tell the future; my voice teacher, Nora, who says she's a sought-after psychic; and the latest addition, Jericho, the prophet. Jericho, my sister's friend, claims to be a prophet of God and receive messages from God. I want so badly to believe that this is possible, but I'm skeptical.

My sister went out with him and came back with prophesies. The first thing out of Jericho's mouth when my sister asked him to talk about me was, "I see a man, light skinned and brown haired. Your sister has a lot of questions about him. God says no. He's got a lot going on in his life, he's confused, and there's illness in his family, and he's just not available for your sister. Your sister is in his way. She needs to get out of the way. She's not going to be the one to show him the way to God. If she's with him, she's not going to show him the way. God says he's a liar. She's not the woman of God for him."

Mind you, my sister *never* mentioned *anything* about me to Jericho, let alone my dating life. Somehow he knew that there was a boy who occupied my life. As soon as I heard this information, my heart sank. Is it true? Should I believe it? This isn't the first time he's been correct, according to my sister. Everything is vague and can be open to interpretation.

Let me just give you a brief background on this boy. The night my sister hung out with him, the night he spoke of the light-skinned boy with brown hair, he saw a boy walk into the club and instantly mentioned to my sister that this boy was surrounded by a "bad" spirit. Okay, so what? He's sensitive to auras. No, there's more. As the boy left the club hours later, with no intention to return, Jericho began praying for his well-being. He continued praying.

As my sister was watching, the boy continued to walk off into the distance. All of a sudden, my sister saw the boy abruptly turn around, from three blocks away, and walk back toward the club, straight for Jericho, as if he was summoned. My sister had to rub her eyes, for fear of her mind playing tricks on her. It was no mirage, the boy walked right up to Jericho and asked a quizzical "Hello?"

Jericho immediately said, "You have a lot of sadness in your life. Your aunt will be healed of whatever it is she is suffering from, and today will be the last day of your depression."

The boy looked at Jericho, said "thank you," and walked off with an air of solace, which he did not have just a few moments before. Strangely odd, don't you think? This could be a sad, sad day for me if I chose to believe Jericho. Lucky for me, I have a strong will. (Actually, I'm not sure how that helps me. In this situation, I think it probably hinders me).

Last thing I do before I go to bed is check my Facebook and the "updates" page. Right there blaring at me was Carter's status: "Branding cattle, covered in cow sh*t in Bovina, TX, with the fam. Seein' Elvis in Memphis, TN. A glass of vino on the sand in Manhattan Beach under the stars with my favorite lady. All in one fun day." That answered my question. He wasn't online because he was still in Texas and hanging out with his "favorite lady." Gross, dude. Save it for each other, not the whole world.

Wednesday, September 8, 2010

I guess I didn't realize how large of a toll Jericho's prophesies took on me. I was sad all day today and wanted to call Rico, who usually consoles me. However, there was no way I was going to call him about another guy, or even pretend that there was something else bothering me just to get his shoulder to cry on.

I'm living such a twisted life. How do I get out of it? I should be careful what I wish for. I'm not sure if I would know what life would be like without drama or Carter. I might just fall into the same obsessive habits with another guy or, worse yet, something illegal. It's like what's said about prisoners. Inmates who have been in prison for too long and get released don't know how to function in the real world.

All they've known for the greater portion of their adult life is within the barbed wire fence of a prison. Many actually commit more crimes just to be sent back to that comfort zone, where they know how to maneuver and "live." That could be me. Wow! I'm a prisoner of my own mind. Is that considered psycho? Do I have a chemical imbalance? Should I be in an insane asylum?

I was sad all day until I told Anna what Jericho said and heard her reaction. She made my day. She instantly said, "You already knew this. You already know that you aren't going to be with Rico, that he's not right for you."

Whoa! I didn't even consider Rico as a candidate for who Jericho was talking about. It's all open to interpretation. Is this boy who Jericho talked about a liar to me? Or to himself? Does he have a physical or mental illness? Is God saying no for right now or no for forever? The time frame is crucial also. So many questions and TOO much time to wallow in my patheticness. (I know it's not a word but I am just that ridiculous that I need to coin a term to describe myself). By the way, Carter was back online today so I changed my Gchat status. I should stop changing my status just for him. Oh, and I'm doing really well with the not checking out his Facebook page. I haven't looked in eight days. Only twenty-two more days to go. I'm almost there. Okay, maybe not, but I need to cheer myself on otherwise I might lose sight of the goal.

Thursday, September 9, 2010

I've been having a lot of dreams about Carter marrying Brook lately. I'm getting insecure and less confident in the fact that he will come back to me.

Friday, September 10, 2010

One of the tutoring families that I'm close with invited me to go with them to Manhattan Beach tomorrow for the day. I want to go! My sister asked, "Would you want to go if they were going to Huntington Beach?" Ugh. She's so smart. Of course not!

I enjoy their company, but I want to go with them because they are going to Manhattan Beach, and there is a slight chance that I would run into, you know, him. I do that a lot—go places in hopes of running into him. It works a lot of the time, but, I know, it's pathetic and loserish and stalkerish. Oh Carter. When will I be through with you?

Saturday, September 11, 2010

I woke up early to meet the inspector for the townhouse I put an offer on back in June. It's been three months since the initial acceptance of my offer. I'm counting down the days until I'm a homeowner. It's so exciting. What's even more exciting is that I'll have big news for Carter, and I'm pretty sure he'll be shocked and impressed and turned on all at the same time.

I was regretting the fact that I declined the offer to go to Manhattan Beach. To make myself feel better, I looked up the temperature and noticed that it was going to be only seventy-five degrees and overcast. I felt better about my decision. I also saw on Gchat that Carter's status was "Riverside." He probably wasn't going to be at the beach anyway.

Today, I was going to purge the superfluous men from my life. I called Ben, the guy who is moving to England but would rather stay here for me, to let him know that we can't hang out. I'm not into him. That was so easy. Why can't I do that with Carter?

I called Reed, the neighbor, and told him that I wasn't interested in him romantically but that I would consider hanging out if that was not an issue with him. (I only said this because I knew for a fact he would decline it). Again, so easy. Tonight I went to a Greek festival in Los Angeles. This is Carter's church festival. He usually goes every year. On the off chance that I might run into him, even though his status said he was in Riverside, I got dressed up. I even put my hair down and wore makeup. Rico came along too. He thought I got all dolled up for him.

I rarely got dressed up for Rico anymore; I was too comfortable around him because I knew he loved me no matter what. In my preoccupation with getting prettied up for Carter, I almost left the picture frame next to my computer with the picture of me and him up. Rico would have had a fit if he saw that. In addition, I left my computer on and left my journaling about Carter on the screen. I was getting sloppy here. It's getting difficult to keep track of who I'm hurting.

Sunday, September 12, 2010

Rico stayed the night, and he explained to me why he was so upset with me at the festival last night. I also invited Noah. All night, he was sizing me up, and Rico didn't appreciate him. Rico was so annoyed with Noah that he contemplated taking a cab back home, but he stayed for me, because he loves me. He's so darn sensitive, but then he makes it up with his absolute love for me. I can do no long-term wrong in his eyes. All will be forgiven.

This morning, after he left, he texted me, "I had a great time. All the crapper head in the world can't spoil the time I spend with you. Besides, all the emotion shows how much you mean to me! XOOX." If I could just combine Rico's love for me with Assface's looks and lifestyle, I would be all set. (As a side note, I was very attracted to Rico, but even more so to Assface). It's never that easy. There is no mixing and matching in romance. It's all or nothing.

I talked to my mom today, and she made it clear to me that she did not want me listening to or believing any of what Jericho, my sister's prophesizing friend, said. Her rationale behind her blatant comment was that the information was completely abstract.

What he said could pertain to Rico or to Carter. I could spend my whole life trying to abide by the prophecy when I didn't even understand it. Even so, knowing what Jericho said wouldn't improve my life.

I have the will of God, and if I honestly have good intentions, then God will give me an opportunity to turn any decision I make into the right path. I have God within me, and that's enough. My mommy is right; moms are always right.

I was even thinking about talking to an astrologer over the phone because my real estate agent mentioned that she spoke to one annually. What was I thinking? My fate is in God's hands and the Holy Spirit within me to guide me to make the best decisions, not a psychic.

By the way, it's been twelve days since I've checked Carter's Facebook. Only eighteen more days to go.

Eric and Alex, Carter's cousins, both called me from the festival today asking me to go again. The festival ran all weekend. They wanted me to go and were naming all the people who were there that I would know. Neither one mentioned Carter, so I wasn't too keen on meeting them, even though I hadn't seen Alex since that day in Manhattan Beach when I saw Carter. They were spying for me without even knowing.

Monday, September 13, 2010

Nothing to report. That's a first. Well, I had nothing to report until later this evening. I was cleaning out my mail drawer downstairs and came across a note that I had written to Carter before the breakup. It was my practice run for what I was going to say on the phone months ago. I was feeling excluded from his life; and I wanted to step up our relationship. Here's the note:

> When we hang out I have a lot of fun and it seems like you have fun too. Whenever I go out or have an event, I usually think to invite you. It seems like you have a lot of activities, but you don't invite me, so I'm confused because if we have fun together, why don't we hang out more?

The day I called to explain all this to him was the day he broke it off with me. I never even had a chance to tell him.

In retrospect, I was feeling excluded because I was *being* excluded on purpose. Carter never fully committed to me and I didn't see that until months later. My eyes were clouded with unrealistic fantasies of Carter that I failed to see the flames. I was slowly being burned, yet I didn't feel the fire until I was scarred. I had let my heart lie in the sun for too long.

Finally, I thought, no more being manipulated for the sole purpose of giving Carter admiration and approval. It's not my love he needs; it's his own.

Unfortunately, my mind and heart were rarely in sync. While I thought I could be strong enough to detach from Carter, my heart felt otherwise, apparent by my next thought.

"I hadn't been contacted by Carter recently. I hope he hasn't forgotten about me." Damn him for monopolizing my brain!

Little did I know what excitement was about to happen.

Tuesday, September 14, 2010

I'd been trying to get to bed at a decent hour every night because I noticed that when I actually got eight hours of sleep, my skin looked good and I felt energetic. I went to bed at around 10:00 p.m. on Monday and was in a deep sleep. All of a sudden, I heard a loud unfamiliar noise. At first, I thought it was my alarm, but when I opened my eyes, it was still pitch dark, and it wasn't the usual sound my alarm made.

I was trying to be as logical as possible in my delirious state. I thought maybe it was my sister's alarm, but the sound was so loud and close to me. I jumped out of bed to go yell at whoever's technology was being obnoxious.

I saw my phone lighting up. What! It's my phone? I've never heard that ring tone before. Then, I looked at the name scrolling on my screen. Carter Swinton. I rubbed my eyes. Was I dreaming? I don't remember this being his ring tone. (But then again, phones do funny stuff when they are being charged).

I was about to pick it up, but then decided against it. It was still ringing. He was calling me!

I picked my phone up again, and I was about to answer, and once again decided against it. All the while this was happening, I was pleading out loud to myself, "I'm bulletproof! I'm bulletproof!" That was my theme song. That's how I can resist temptation. It was my mantra until I got strong enough to resist without assistance.

Just last night, didn't I make the decision to disconnect from Carter? The strength I had yesterday vanished; Carter's hold on me is too strong.

This was too difficult. He was right there at my fingertips, calling me, and I was available, but I wasn't picking up.

I was rationalizing the wrong way. I was trying to talk myself out of picking up the phone, but instead, I was finding more reasons to pick it up. In a frantic craze, I ran to my sister's room.

Don't ask me why I did that or what I was expecting to happen. I just needed to be away from my cell phone.

For some reason, she was awake, as if she were in on the plan and wanted to see my reaction. I had to stay in her room until the phone stopped ringing, which seemed like an eternity. She was trying to calm me down. I was in the middle of telling her that Carter was calling and that he never leaves messages when all of a sudden, I heard, "Breaking news!" (That's what I say every time I hear the alert for a voice mail). What?!

He left a message. I ran to my phone, checked the time, 1:48 a.m., ran back to my sister's room, and listened to the voice mail on speaker phone. We listened to the message twice, trying to analyze all the nuances of his voice and what he was saying. I had been dead tired, but now I was wide awake. Only he was capable of making me giddy in the middle of the night, especially on a work night. Here's what he said:

> "Hey there, it's Carter. It's about, uh kind of early, about one forty-five. Just driving home. I was up in downtown LA and was listening to some country music and I guess there was some song that uh made me feel like calling and saying hello, and just uh wishing you well. I hope things are going fine and um ya, have a good week. Bye."

I wanted to scream out of happiness. All I could think was, *It's not over! It's not over! He's thinking about me.* So many thoughts were rushing through my mind. The flood gates were wide open. He still had a girlfriend, yet he was calling me at a very late hour of the night. That's not fair to her. It must mean that he isn't that committed.

He wanted me. He was very detailed in the message. He didn't have to tell me about the song. He said "uhm" a lot. This calculated boy never said "uhm." Or was that part of the calculation? He wanted me. This made me happy. Maybe now I finally had the upper hand. Should I call back? What do I do? I really want to know what song reminded him of me.

My momentary sanity kicked in reminding me that Carter was a psychological vampire, attaching to me and draining my mental and emotional resources. The mental gymnastics I had to perform just to keep up with Carter were making me question my worth and even my sanity.

Pushing any rational thoughts aside, I rushed to the computer to check the playlist on Los Angeles's only country station at 1:45 a.m. shortly before he called, to see what song he possibly could have been listening to at that hour of the night. It was Reba McEntire's song, "Somebody." Interesting. That's not a song that was special to us.

The impractical questioning went on for hours. I tried to go back to sleep but couldn't fall asleep until 5:00 a.m., only to be woken up by my alarm an hour later. Needless to say, my efforts of trying to go to bed early were useless because I was dead tired the next day, but giddy. This morning, before leaving for work, my groggy sister insisted, "Don't call him back. He was calling too late just to say hi. Maybe if he called during the day, it would be more appropriate for you to call. Just don't do anything."

I told my dad, and he said, "I told you he'd come back. But this still isn't enough. He's still not trying hard enough. Don't contact him." I told my mom the events of the night. She said, "You're going to marry him. It's just a matter of when. He cares about you, there's no question about that. He still isn't doing anything with that, though."

At work, I told my second mommy, Maggie. She said, "Sometimes God tests us to the max. But the devil also tests us. You have to decide who's putting you to the test. You know the answer to this, I'm sure. I love you, Lily."

I told Yvonne, and she said, "Lily, don't let him slip on by. If you love him, go after him. Don't play games. This is why I'm in the situation I'm in right now with my husband and Andy. I love

Andy and want to be with him, but he confessed to me too late that he loved me. If I had only shared with him how I felt years ago, I would probably be married to him, much more happily than I am with Frank. Don't be an idiot, Lily. Go after what you want before it's too late."

I told Cassie, Robert, and Ava, the Manhattan Beach family, and they said, "You need to rid your life of him. Even if he called you at that hour in the past, it's out of context now and is completely inappropriate. You should pick up the phone next time and call him out on his two-timing. You need to let him know that you don't want anything to do with him unless he wants you for good. Just by you ignoring all his attempts to contact you, you're still enabling him. You haven't given him a definite 'no' signal. Get rid of him, Lily. We're looking for eligible men for you."

I told Anna, and she said, "Songs are relevant when you want them to be, but it's interesting that he called just to tell you at 2:00 a.m. It's pretty crazy he called when he has a girlfriend. You still shouldn't contact him. He's not trying hard enough. If he really wants you in his life, then he won't be deterred by you ignoring him for little things like this. Besides, he didn't ask you to call him back."

I told Eric, his cousin, and he said, "Clearly, he loves you. You're one of his closest friends, and he can count on you. If he's calling you, it's because you fulfill something on some level that his girlfriend doesn't fulfill. He knows you get him better than anyone else."

So that's great and all, but what am I supposed to do with that? Wait forever? Be a best friend to the man I'm in love with and throw out my emotions simply for his convenience? I *didn't* tell Nora, my psychic voice teacher, and she said as soon as she saw me, "How's Carter? Did he call you? I've been sending messages out to the universe for him to come back to you. I've really been putting it out there. This is a good sign that he called.

I'll keep sending messages out, but I will only do it a few more times because if I do it too much, he might reject the message. You should do whatever your heart tells you to do. You know him better than anyone else. Trust your instinct. Trust your gut."

Whatever mumbo jumbo silliness she was saying was fine with me if it was in my favor. Maybe she really was psychic. I don't know. So many different opinions, and no one really knew him. All I wanted to do was talk to him. I just wanted to text him, maybe sometime next week late at night. "What song?" I'm like Dennis the Menace with my phone. It's too hard for me to hold my fingers back. They're itching to text or call Carter. Pretty soon I was going to need a restraint. My whole universe was a Carter ordeal.

Wednesday, September 15, 2010

My sister had her friend Danny stay over last night. Our bedrooms share a wall, so she can hear pretty much everything. Last night, I recorded Carter's message onto a tape. Every voice mail that Carter had ever left me from the past ten years was on this tape. I was trying to transcribe the message for my journaling, but I was having a hard time catching everything he was saying.

I wanted to get it exactly right with all his "uhms" and "uhs." I listened to the message at least fourteen times. Analyzing and reanalyzing.

Danny officially thought I was crazy and sickly obsessed. He already thought I was crazy, but now it was over the top. Oh well. I was entertaining, I guess.

Thursday, September 16, 2010

The book I was reading talked about love frequently. *The Pilgrimage*, by Paulo Coelho, differentiated between three types of love. *Agape* is the Greek word for the highest and purest form of love, one that surpasses all other types of affection, the love that consumes. Many people experience *eros*, the Greek word for intimate, lustful love. Others only experience *philos*, the love of friendship and respect.

Most people can't differentiate between agape and eros and usually mistake eros, sexual attraction and intimacy, for agape, true love.

Coelho writes that enthusiasm toward a particular goal is agape. When we love and believe deeply, we feel ourselves to be stronger than anyone in the world, and nothing can shake the certainty of our faith.

This is exactly how I felt about Carter. Nothing could get in my way. My enthusiasm for my ultimate goal, to be with Carter, consumed me.

I find it refreshing to be able to love with such entirety, and I'm thankful for the opportunity to love wholly despite the pain it has brought me. I wouldn't want to leave this earth not knowing the feeling of absolute true love. I would rather love than not love at all. Hopefully, that consuming love will be returned by Carter.

Friday, September 17, 2010

"The people who need love and compassion the most are often the ones who deserve it the least." That was Carter's Facebook status that came up on my "updates" page. Self-description right there. He needed love and compassion the most but deserved it the least. Assface.

Saturday, September 18, 2010

I had a dream about Carter again. They're becoming more frequent, not better though. My subconscious was really trying to speak to me these days.

I dreamt that we were being physical, of course in secret, with his friends nearby not knowing anything. We were about to have sex, and he stopped it and said we couldn't. It wasn't right. "I can't be with you, so we can't do this," he said. So I left the room, but he came back minutes later and started kissing me and turning me on. I assumed he'd changed his mind, and it got to that sexy point again, and he firmly said, "No."

Annoyed, I said, "You can't play around with me like this. It's all or nothing. I can't be your friend. I want to be with you. I love you. There is no in between." Then I started laughing, looked at him the same way a child tries to make sense of something new, and said, "You and I are so alike. What you do to me is what I do to Rico. I can't blame you for being the way you are because I'm the same, and it's hard not to be that way."

Waking up to karma biting you in the butt is not pleasant. For once, my dream was pretty self-explanatory. Since I couldn't admit in reality that I take advantage of Rico, my guilt seeped into my subconscious and revealed itself. At some point, I had to face my denial. Even though I still stick to my gut that Carter loves me, he was still using me for his ego, just like I was using Rico. I was paying forward the wrong action.

Anna and I talk just about every day. We both know that our friendship is a rarity. We have a very open and honest relationship. We never get sick of each other, and we always make each other laugh. The only problem is that we don't enjoy the same activities.

We talk on the phone a lot, but we don't do much outside of that, which is unfortunate because we love each other. We were talking about that and how it's truly important to marry your best friend who enjoys the same interests. I mentioned that that's why I love Carter. He loves to do what I love to do.

Then I stood on my soapbox for a brief moment. "Anna, there is not one day that I have not thought about Assface since I met him. Do you realize how much time that is? That's more than 3,650 days, more than 87,600 hours. Every morning, he's the first thing I think about. Every night, he's the last thing I think about."

In shock, Anna responded by getting on a soapbox of her own and exclaimed, "Oh my gosh! That's a lot of time. I just hope that that time is being put into use for the future. I just want you to try having part of your life without him and see what happens. It's like the past ten years you've been on hold, and I just want you to press Play. You've done everything you're supposed to do to get over someone. You've gone by the book, but that's exactly it—by the book. That's not hard enough. Of course you can't stop yourself from thinking about him, but stop making him the center of your life. Right now, he's dead center. You constantly talk about him with other people, strangers even. You need to try harder not to do that.

Haven't you ever heard that if you love something, let it go, and if it comes back, then it's true? Just let fate take its path instead of trying to be a control freak by making things happen. Bottom line: Try not to make him the center of your life. I just want you to be happy."

See, this is why I love her. She's done this for the past ten years. She only knew me for one year before I met Carter and turned to her for support. She could have dropped out years ago, but she stuck around. Where others fell silent, she never ran out of wise advice.

Anna seriously is such a great friend. She saw the pain in my eyes while everyone else still believed in the smile on my face. Drama usually ends. She knew that my drama didn't have an end date. Mine just kept going like the Energizer bunny, and she just kept taking the beating, the loudass drumming. Maybe she should wear a wedding dress at my wedding too, if I marry Assface. It's partially her relationship.

After all that great advice, all I could think was why God had Carter and me meet. The only reason I went to camp the year I met Assface was because my mom randomly saw a job description for a counselor position at a church camp in our church bulletin. It all boils down to my mom.

But what's interesting about this is that my church never advertises for that camp. It always advertises for another camp. And every year afterward, I would always look to see if they ever advertised that position again. Never! And that was also the *only* year Assface was a counselor. Funny how things work. God for sure wanted us to meet. But as for the outcome, it's still not certain what God wanted.

Sunday, September 19, 2010

I tutored many of the kids at my church. Over the years, I've built relationships with the mothers, and for some reason, they all love me. They all looked out for me and were always looking for eligible bachelors for me.

Today, at my church's Greek festival, when I ran into them, they started rattling off compliments and telling me how great I looked. They started talking about who they could set me up with. They were always trying to marry me off. I think it's funny and flattering.

That same night at the festival, I ran into Drake, a longtime acquaintance. I hadn't seen him in years, but I knew. I knew that he instantly took a liking to me, and I could tell that he was trying to flirt. He wasn't very good at it though. He was totally digging me.

As if that weren't enough, Marco Patren, a guy I met doing competitive Greek dancing, was totally trying to get my attention and dance with me. Proof once again that I'm charming and that I can get any guy I want, except Carter Swinton.

My favorite part of the Greek festivals was the dancing. Greek line dancing both satisfied my need to dance and my need to avoid awkward men. Glad that Greek line dancing didn't require partner dancing, it was easy to step away from my admirers.

People jumped in and out of the lines as their energy levels fluctuated. Concentrating on learning the footwork to a new dance, I didn't notice Carter Vantillon jump in and grab my hand. I momentarily lost my concentration when I realized who he was.

It was so cool that it was him. In the past, we had a short tryst and he disappeared. I never got closure or understood what exactly happened. One look into his eyes, and I knew he was nervous to be around me. He was a wreck. Seemed like he had been out of the dating world for years.

Now this was one boy I would step out of the dance line for. But, every time I tried to pull both of us out to attempt to have a conversation somewhere quiet, he reeled me back in with such force, I felt like I was getting whiplash. So, I just danced.

Despite the volume of the music, he tried to make conversation with me while dancing. Who makes conversation when they are dancing?

Great, three very non-smooth guys. That's totally not my style, but for some reason, Carter Vantillon stood out to me and momentarily made me forget about Carter Swinton. Later on in the evening, Eric came for the last hour of the festival. He knew a lot of people whom I didn't know. He introduced me to one girl in particular, Erica Tas, who happened to be Carter's childhood neighbor for seventeen years.

Why is everyone connected to Carter? Or am I just finding connections? I truly feel like there is a thread connecting us together. It's thick enough that I can't cut it. The question is why does it still exist, and when will it ever get threadbare?

As if that weren't enough, I ran into an ex-girlfriend of his. She gave me her number and said we should hang out. Does the Carter in my life ever subside? What an exhausting night.

Monday, September 20, 2010

Yvonne and I gossiped about boys at work today. That's what we do best. By the way, I still haven't checked Carter's Facebook. Only ten more days. I heard back from my loan officer and real estate agent about my townhouse. The loan officer asked for an extension from the banks to have time to fund the loans. Reluctantly, both banks agreed to extend the closing date for escrow to October 15 instead of September 30, but with no further extensions.

My real estate agent explained to me that if things didn't go through, it was very possible that the home would go into foreclosure and that it would go back on the market into an auction. All the paperwork, time and processes I went through since June would be erased. None of it would matter. It was all getting cut so close. I was getting nervous.

Despite all the delay, I had a good feeling about this. I think I'll get it. But, what do I know about feelings? I thought I knew that Carter was the one for me. I was so sure of it, but nothing has come of that. I don't even know if I can trust my instincts anymore. I'm so confused.

Tuesday, September 21, 2010

I had a talk with Anna today, and she said, "Deep, deep, deep, deep down, I'm still team Assface. But he needs to prove it to you."

I was reading through my journaling and came across the only clock time I mentioned in writing. I mentioned that I was journaling at 1:48 a.m. How ironic that that is the exact time that Carter called me the other night. Is that a thread or a crazy coincidence? Either way, it's pretty crazy.

Last night, I sent myself an e-mail with the subject "Yvonne Swinton." I made that the subject because it was supposed to be a reminder to tell Yvonne about Carter. Listen to how ridiculous

I was. I opened my e-mail today and saw the boldface, "Yvonne Swinton," subject line and got jealous. *Who is this Yvonne Swinton?* I swear sometimes I'm so absurd. I got jealous of my own message.

Wednesday, September 22, 2010

Carter instant messaged me that afternoon.

> Carter: ur friends with erica now?
> Me: yes
> Carter: she's nice. I'm sure u 2 talked about curly hair
> Me: what song was it?
> Carter: it was rascal flats, my wish. wen'd u meet Erica?
> Me: my church greek fest
> Carter: somehow I managed to miss all the greekfests this year
> Me: not surprising...you're always busy
> Carter: maybe cuz I thought I'd ruin ur day if u saw me. you're always busy
> Me: why would you ruin my day?
> Carter: cuz ur upset with me and don't want to see/talk to me. I don't know...u don't talk to me ever anymore
> Me: I'm a lot of things with you but not upset.
> *Seriously, Lily? You're being manipulated again. He barely turned on the inaudible charm and I hear it as a blast*
> Carter: a lot of things with me? you care to elaborate?
> Me: more than anything, I'm hurt for many reasons...too much to type, if you want to know you can call. there's a lot going on in your life and you need to figure it out without me in it as any sort of distraction. To be honest, I thought it was inappropriate for you to call me so late at night, especially when you have a girlfriend and considering our recent past
> Carter: really? um, sorry. ur always up late and I was just making a friendly call hello. it wasn't a "distraction" and didn't have anything to do with whatever went on in our past. I don't see any difference calling u then or

calling you at 6pm. I don't see u as a distraction. I'm sorry you feel hurt, and I would like to discuss that with you wen u'd like. It's been like 4 months since I've seen you, and we've talked maybe twice in this whole time. I would think some hurt or whatever emotion would subside by now.

Once again, Carter, you flipped my world upside down. How about just saying, "hello." How about just asking me about my day. Why start the conversation with an agenda?

I'm not sure how to feel about this conversation. He noticed that I'm friends with Erica, which means he had to see something on my Facebook. Is he trying to make conversation with me, or is he upset, like I'm invading his life? The song that reminded him of me was definitely an interesting choice. Here are some lines that stand out to me.

"More than anything, more than anything, my wish, for you, is that this life becomes all that you want it to. And while you're out there getting where you're getting to, I hope you know somebody loves you, and wants the same things too."

What I get from this is that he loves me, but from a distance. Like he's telling me to move on because our parallel lives won't cross. It has the *L* word (love) in it, so it's throwing me off. What am I supposed to think? Am I reading too much into it? Then, there's the fact that he wants to talk about my feelings. That's new. Since when was he genuinely interested in how I feel? I don't think he truly understands how deeply I care for him and how hurt I am.

Thursday, September 23, 2010

I heard a noise I would recognize anywhere. It was the sound of a text message alert from Carter. (Remember that his is personalized. It's different than everyone else's). My heart started racing. But wait. My phone is on vibrate. It can't be mine. What a letdown. It was my student Samantha's, phone. I'm so ridiculous.

Shortly after that episode, he called at 11:05 a.m., while I was teaching. There are no cell phones allowed in class, including my own. Yet, I didn't say a word to Samantha about her incoming text because her alert was a Carter reminder, and I picked up my phone during class because it was Carter.

I guess he really wanted to talk about my feelings. I stayed calm and collected until I apologized for not talking about my feelings with him yesterday. Why was I apologizing? What was this power I had given him, that I bow down to anything Carter?

I told him I'd call him later when I wasn't in the middle of teaching to discuss my thoughts. Why was he insistent on hearing my side? I was going to have to be prepared to say exactly how I feel once and for all. There's no way I can do that without preparing. I'll have to write a letter and read it to him. This was going to be my one shot to explain everything to him.

Friday, September 24, 2010

My sister, mom, and I left for a mini weekend vacation in Desert Springs. In the car, I explained to my mommy and my sister what my game plan was going to be. I practiced what I would say to Carter. I was so emotional I cried. I was truly trying to be optimistic about the whole situation.

Telling Carter everything would mean that I could finally get him out of my system and start a new chapter in my life. I was so scared. This could mean losing him forever. Unfortunately, the wisest decisions are not always the easiest ones.

I could easily just continue this haphazard relationship with him and stay stagnant. But is that what I really want? I want him to have all the facts, and I want the ball to clearly be in his court. I want to be able to say that I did all that I could. I have to do this.

Saturday, September 25, 2010

What a welcoming day today was, considering the sadness I was feeling in the car yesterday. I went golfing for the first time in my life, and it was a disaster. I figured I should try the sport since I was in Desert Springs, and that's pretty much all there is to do there. When in Rome.

It was a hilarious experience. I did everything wrong and disregarded every rule of golf etiquette unintentionally. I wouldn't have been surprised if I made it into the news as the one-hundred-pound girl who terrorized the golf course in Desert Springs.

First, I was wearing the wrong attire: short, cut-off jean shorts and a bright purple and pink tie-dye tank top. They weren't going to let me golf, but I convinced them to. I had no idea what I was doing or where to start, and I was just wandering the course. At the first hole, I drove the golf cart onto the green and got reprimanded by a group of golfers, who I swear appeared out of nowhere, telling me that I was breaking the number one rule of golf.

At the second hole, I hit the ball onto the wrong course and got reprimanded, again. The course was confusing me, and the concrete car path, stopped. I didn't know where to go and ended up driving through a few people's games and, of course, got reprimanded.

Rushing to get out of people's ways, I almost tipped the golf cart over, which I didn't even know was possible. Worst of all, at the fourth hole, I hit the golf ball into the sliding glass doors of a condo. The first thing I thought was, *I hope none of the golfers who've been reprimanding me saw that, because I've had enough scolding for the day.*

After I hit the condo, I called it a day. I also understood why errant golf ball insurance was part of buying a home paperwork, something I had haughtily laughed about when signing my home loan contract. That was only the fourth hole.

I was laughing so hard I was crying the entire two hours I was on the golf course. Definitely not my sport.

Sunday, September 26, 2010

All day today, I wrote and rewrote and rewrote what I would say to Carter. Like I said earlier, this was my one shot to get everything off my chest, to release all my demons. I could very easily just ignore the guy and call it a day, but as my favorite author, Paulo Coelho, says, fleeing from a battle is worse than losing a fight because you can always learn something from defeat; but if you flee you've let the enemy win.

Not to say that Carter is my enemy, but the whole situation is a disservice to my life. I can't move on because I have too many "what if" scenarios. I just want all the cards laid out on the table once and for all.

All day my heart was beating. I was getting nervous. It was almost time. Every time I went to call, my phone would ring. It's almost like I wasn't meant to call. *Why, God, are you prolonging this?* At about 10:30 p.m., I gave him a call. He didn't answer, and I was prepared for that. I had a message planned out. "Hey I'm calling to talk. If you get this message today, I'll be up late. If I don't hear from you, I'll try calling you tomorrow."

No call from him that night. I had very restless sleep.

Monday, September 27, 2010

I had a good day at work today. I was feeling quite prepared for tonight. My dad would always say, "You only need thirty seconds of courage, then it's all over." This was going to be a very long thirty seconds. At 9:38 p.m., I called him again. He picked up. Here's what I said. I recorded it too. I'm not sure why, but I did.

So I'm going to be completely honest about everything. I'm going to explain to you why I'm hurt and where it all stems from. I have a lot to say, so please just let me say everything before you comment. I'm not going to pretend that this is easy. It's actually very difficult for me. I had to write it down. I didn't want to leave anything out, so I'm going to read it to you. So the other day, you were saying how all the emotions should have subsided by now, and they have, but I don't think you understand the intensity of my feelings. You've always known that I care about you, that I care a lot, but I don't think you know that I love you. I don't mean to bring up past relationships, but I want to give you a point of reference. How you felt about Lauren, or at least how you portrayed it to me is how I feel about you. When Lauren was in your life, I didn't exist to you. You cared about her so much you didn't even want to be my friend. During that time, I tried to build a friendship, hang out, call, and you chose to ignore my attempts. Now when it's the most inappropriate time, you're trying to be my friend. I'm getting mixed signals. I'm tired of the hot and cold, the stringing along, the leading on. I'm tired of being the back burner girl. It's exhausting. If we were truly just friends, then I wouldn't be hurt by your actions. But that's not the case because I love you. You're probably wondering how I can love you without us ever seriously dating. I've had that same question many times when guys profess their love for me after one or two dates. I understand now. Love is funny like that. When you know, you know.

Four, five months ago when we started hanging out again, I was going into it simply for fun. I had my guard up because you told me before you weren't interested. That was my mind-set. But you turned it into something more, so I dropped my guard and went along with it. I was at my most vulnerable state, Carter. You started taking an interest in my life, sent me a picture because it reminded you of me, initiated talks about marriage and babies, even if you were just joking. My experience is that anything said in a joke is also a half-serious comment. You made it clear that you were thinking about me, which led me to believe you felt as strongly as I did. So when you told me that you met another girl who's more about you than I am, I was shocked and hurt. My first reaction was, how can the intense feelings you were leading me to believe disappear in a moment? How can some girl replace me so quickly? Like I said, I originally went into it with a "just for now" attitude, and you made it seem like it could be "more than just for now." Of course, I was brutally hurt. All of the emotions I felt then have gone away, except for the hurt, simply because I care too much. You can't explain love. Here I am putting myself out there, showing my vulnerability, and for what? Just so you understand where I'm coming from and that I can't be a game to you. You've always had the upper hand with me, and you've known that quite well. But I'm tired of being the lower hand. I'm usually the one fighting guys off. I'm the one with the upper hand, always, except with you. I get that both positions are no fun. It's hard to make the right choice, the one that doesn't lead the other person on, if you care about them at all. I'm not mad at you, I'm not upset with you, I'll never hate you, I have no negativity toward you. I want you to be happy, but I'd prefer that you be happy with me. If I'm not with you, I don't know that I can be your friend. I don't want to see you with other girls. I truly want to be your friend, but with how intensely I feel for you and how you don't feel about me, I don't think it's possible. I hope you can respect that. I don't mind if I run into you, but I won't actively try to be a part of your life. It's too difficult for me. Bottom line, I'm not attacking you, I don't hate you, I just want you to fully grasp my side. I don't regret any part of our relationship. If anything, I'm blessed to have met you and had the opportunity to feel the way I do.

It's rare to love this intensely. Just know that I care about you. Maybe down the road, our paths will cross. So there it is. The last ten years in a nutshell.

Surprisingly, I didn't cry. Here's his response:

Okay. Without thinking too much, here's what comes to mind. I never meant to hurt you, or play games with you. Over the years, there were times when we got along, and things were good, and then I would retreat a bit, but it wasn't a game to me. That's just how it was. The last few months when we were hanging out, I didn't mean to replace you. I'm sorry that I hurt you so much, but it wasn't intentional. It just so happened that I met this girl very accidentally, and I knew 100 percent that she's right for me. I knew that I found a good thing. I wasn't 100 percent sure with you. For one thing, we have different mind-sets and beliefs. I will never date another Christian girl again. It's nice to be on the same page with this girl. I was able to call and text you the last few months knowing for a fact that you are just my friend because I'm in love with her. In the past, I messaged you flirting. I didn't mean to give you mixed signals.

Forty-nine minutes later, the Carter Swinton extended version chapter was finally put to a close. I didn't cry, not one tear. Instead, I was in a surreal state. How you're supposed to feel when you're the happiest person alive, walking on air, is how I felt that night. I was walking around in a haze, lightheaded and weightless, but not because I was at all happy.

I don't even think I can describe what I was feeling. I just know that it was a very strange feeling, something I've never felt before. It was weird. After careful consideration, it crossed my mind that maybe I really was happy. Maybe my soul was relieved to finally let go of this damper on my life.

I have heard that it is in the hard times when you experience the love of God the most intensely. In my deepest pain, I know that God is holding me together, and His heart breaks along with mine. I found solace in that thought.

Why don't men follow directions? It's impossible for them to consider anyone but themselves. Fifteen minutes after the phone conversation, he texted me, "Thanks for talking with me. Please take care."

Was that necessary? We already said our good-byes on the phone, and I specifically told him to give me my space and leave me alone. Did he really have to go and open the wound again so soon? I was trying to make the story end, and he wouldn't let me.

The irony of my life was too comical. How could I be upset with Carter for leading me on when I was doing the exact same thing to Rico? I knew he loved me and would catch a grenade for me simply to be in my presence. Even though Rico and I were supposed to spend the entire next weekend together, I decided to be unselfish for a moment and do the right thing. The correct route isn't always the easiest.

But learning can't happen without change. Life would be stagnant.

I've heard it many times before but never fully understood the meaning of it until recently. "What doesn't kill you only makes you stronger." So I called Rico that night, mustered the little strength I had left, and told him that I didn't want to be selfish anymore and I didn't want to hurt him anymore. I knew deep down that he was not the man for me and spending time together was spiraling us in the wrong direction.

He agreed with me and said that even though we were allowed to date other people, he was emotionally unavailable to any other woman because he cared about me tremendously. He admitted that if I never said anything, he would have let this pattern continue for a very long time despite the fact that he has felt like he was my one-night stand for the last three years.

That comment confirmed that I was doing the right thing. It was a horrible feeling. I guess love can make you do crazy things.

I am his Carter, his Achilles' heel, the chink in his armor, his Kryptonite. I completely understand the situation he's in.

I also would have let Carter and me go on forever simply to be in his presence even though I knew he didn't feel the same way.

I did, and even though I knew I was being used. I love Rico, but not for marriage. I know Carter loves me, but not for marriage.

That phone call to Rico took a harder toll on me than the call to Carter. I was sobbing hysterically after I got off the phone. It's harder to be in the position of letting someone go, because you feel guilty. I know that with Rico, what happens with us is in my hands.

However, with Carter, I did all I could. I've thrown my hands up; there wasn't much more I could do, so the situation wasn't as tormenting to me. I can't force him to love me just like I can't force myself to love Rico. Even though Rico is a man who would go to the ends of the earth for me, I don't want him, because he's not Carter. I want the asshole who replaced me instantaneously.

After the phone call with Rico, I was tempted to text him and immediately thought, *I am the female version of Carter. I break men's hearts, and I know I'm doing it. I just play dumb.*

I was so good at creating problems. But over the last ten years, I've finally gained a bit of wisdom. Life's problems are something like this: Hold them for a few minutes in your head, and they seem okay. Think of them for a long time, and they begin to ache.

Hold them even longer, and they begin to paralyze you. Carter and Rico were paralyzing me. I wasn't able to do anything. The solution: put the problem down. I think I finally did. Two heart-wrenching phone calls. Two wounds that can finally heal. Two closed doors that will lead to two open doors. There was no need to try to beat down these doors.

I texted my boss at 11:30 that night, telling him I wouldn't be able to make it to work. In all my seven years of work, I've *never* taken a day off unless I was truly sick or on vacation. This was the first time I ever took a mental health day, because I was absolutely emotionally distraught.

From a young age, it's been instilled in me to fight for something wholeheartedly; otherwise, there is zero chance that it can happen. I suppose that I just have to accept the definition of true love that I so adamantly tried to avoid: true love is neither physical nor romantic; it is an acceptance of all that is, that has been, that will, or even *will not be*. To love another person so deeply is to see the face of God. That's what I have to tell myself, that I had a rare opportunity to feel what many do not feel in their lifetime.

Finally, I see that my nostalgia for the better days I had with Carter was just denial of my painful present. I had to choose between life and fiction; the two are very close but never touch. Ultimately, after much pain, I was ready to get in touch with reality, take off my rose colored glasses and start living in the real world. No more protective layers to guard my heart.

Carter, you are my Kryptonite. I loved you yesterday, Carter. I love you still, I always have, and I always will, but I don't like you right now, yet you still manage to affect me. I'm mad at myself, not you. I'm mad for always being nice. I'm mad for always apologizing for things I didn't do. I'm mad for getting attached. I'm mad for depending on you and wasting my time on you. I'm mad for thinking about you and, most of all, for not hating you when I should. I've rounded my edges as much as I can to fit into your square, and somehow I still didn't fit. I guess you were never mine to lose.

Look what you've done to me, Carter Swinton.

Tuesday, September 28, 2010

On my day off, I prayed and reflected and summoned the strength to get out of bed and be productive. Despite my extreme pain, I feel that God is absolutely on my side and looking out for me. That same day, I got a phone call from my loan officer and real estate agent saying that the loan would be funded and escrow would close on the townhouse that I've been trying to get since May. While I was at home, recovering from all the built-up pain and hurt, God gave me a major blessing.

There is no way that timing is that efficient without God. The day I needed good news the most is the day it came to me. He was turning my mourning into dancing. I could feel the sweetness of His love piercing my darkness.

Then I thought about the message from church on Sunday and couldn't think of a more fitting sermon for my situation. During the biblical times, the year of the Jubilee was a grand event that was supposed to happen every fifty years. At the beginning of the fiftieth year, everyone was essentially supposed to get a do-over. All debts should be erased, and all slaves should be released.

However, this rule was not followed, and many people were furious. The year of the Jubilee was a year when everyone would become rich again and have a fresh start. Instead of getting a clean slate, many people got nothing at all and were left with debt they thought would be erased.

The prophet Isaiah took this opportunity to give people guidance. Essentially, what he said was, "You have nothing (sympathetically), or you have nothing (excitedly)! This should be a time to celebrate and praise God. Turn your despair into gladness."

I can look at this situation as an extreme loss. I have nothing (feeling sorry for myself), or I can look at it as a do-over with Carter out of my mind, clearing up space for new memories. I have nothing (with excitement). Instead of groaning about what I think I need, I should try to see it from God's perspective.

With that, I smiled for the first time in twenty-four hours. I love you, God.

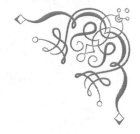

Chapter 20

I had plenty of friends who were proud of me for taking a giant step in the right direction. Life will go on even though I've had my reservations in the past. I know now: "I have nothing!" Maybe now I can pick up the pieces of my shattered heart and move on with my life. Tomorrow is a new day, and I will "rise and shine and give God my glory."

Whenever I feel good about my situation, I come across information that compliments my attitude. Francis Chan, a Christian author wrote that joy is a choice that we have to work for. It doesn't come automatically, just like the ability to run for hours on end. It needs cultivation.

Although it may seem that these pearls of wisdom are ten years too late, the fact is that I would have overlooked the sage words and never thought twice about their implications.

Truly, God has perfect timing. I was waiting so patiently for Carter Swinton to whisk me off my feet and bring joy to my life. I was waiting for the impossible. I chose the joy I wanted but didn't work for it. I was waiting for it to come to me. It's no wonder that Carter Swinton brought me misery rather than joy.

Along the same lines, Francis Chan stated that healing and receiving freedom in answer to prayer is not usually something done to you, where you wait passively. Rather, you are an active participant in your journey to wholeness. God is certainly capable of freeing us from our pain, but asks us to be active participants in the healing process. Often, freedom and healing take time, a very long time. We must learn to persevere just as the runner trains endlessly to be able to run long distances painlessly. Simply praying or looking at the treadmill is a dead end. We must contribute to our lives.

I was just staring at Carter Swinton. I was waiting for him to pounce on the opportunity of me. He was my paper promise to myself. I'll have him one day. How can God even begin to free me of Carter Swinton if I don't want to be freed or don't even have an open mind?

I'm finally truly ready to make a change in my life. Lead me, God. I can't do this alone. Simply telling myself that I was ready for a change and sincerely wanting the change was all it took for God to bank on that opportunity.

Chapter 21

I t just so happened that the upcoming weekend, in early November, I was invited to go to a church retreat in Dunlap, California, to visit a monastery and hear the Word of God. Surprisingly, I was available to go. (I'm always booked to the point where my friends reserve me months in advance). I went on the retreat, not knowing anyone, and preferring it that way.

Ironically, it turned out that the priest leading the retreat was Carter Swinton's second cousin. I really can't get away from him. No matter. I wasn't going to let that distract me from what I came to do, which was be with God.

We got there Friday night and got up early for church Saturday morning. I was looking forward to taking communion at the monastery service. So when I started getting lightheaded during church, I genuinely thought it was odd. I never get lightheaded. I felt so dizzy. Sitting down didn't even help.

I had to leave church for a breath of fresh air. After walking in and out of the church two or three times, I didn't know what to think. It wasn't lack of sleep or food. Finally, it was time for communion; it couldn't come soon enough. As I was walking to get in line for communion, I had this overwhelming feeling of nausea.

I immediately walked out of church. My vision started tunneling, and I was tripping over my steps. I could feel myself blacking out. To avoid getting hurt, I immediately dropped to the ground, face flat, and just lay there in front of the church, sprawled on the ground.

Anyone who would have seen me would have thought I was dead. But because I wasn't dead, it was actually quite comical. A girl dressed in fancy church clothes sprawled, spread-eagle, face down on the ground directly in front of the monastery doors, with the church service going on inside. I didn't know what to do. I genuinely wanted to take communion, but I felt so weak.

After a few minutes, I got up with what little strength I could gather to go back inside. What? The doors that I had come in and out of repeatedly just minutes before were locked. How can that be possible? Unbelievable! I just wanted communion.

Finally, someone opened the door for me. And guess what? Communion was just ending. Oh, and I felt fine. No feeling of dizziness, nausea or lightheadedness whatsoever. Try and explain that. I couldn't, at least not for the better part of the morning.

Church ended without me getting communion. I took a solitary walk to try to sort through the events of the morning. I came up with three options: (1) It was a coincidence that I wasn't feeling well and got locked out of church at the exact moment of communion and got let back in immediately afterward with no sign of sickness. (2) The devil was playing with me. (3) God just didn't want me to take communion today. I went with the latter explanation.

God directly spoke to me that morning. I'm such a stubborn woman. I want what I want and don't always include God. What kind of life is that? I wanted communion so badly; I didn't even care to abide by the rules of sanctity required. You need to confess and repent of your sins each week, and I had sinned badly that week with no sign of remorse.

Yet I was adamant to get the holy body and blood of Christ in my unworthy body. God had to bring me to the ground, facedown, the lowest of the low, and shame me in front of a very holy place in order for Him to get the message across to me loud and clear. "You are not worthy of taking communion today."

The instant I came to that conclusion, I became so emotional I started tearing up. All I could think was, *God, I've let you down. How did I let my life come to this?* I've drifted so far away from where I should be, and part of my drifting had to do with Carter Swinton. Deep down, I always knew that Carter, the guy who was baptized and raised Orthodox Christian and denounced the faith, was bad news for me. But, I never wanted to believe it.

Looking back at some of the events that took place over the last ten years, it was clear to me that Carter Swinton and I were not meant to be together. God gave me signs all the time. I just refused to believe them and instead wondered, *Why, God, why won't you give me who I want?* Now I know—because who I want wasn't necessarily who I need. I get it now.

How in the world could someone like that be an asset to my life and help me glorify God? I guess my sister's prophetic friend was right that I would not be the woman to lead him to God. As the famous country singer Garth Brooks sings, "Thank God for unanswered prayers."

Chapter 22

That moment was a turning point in my life. I could feel the beginning of a new chapter coming on. I finally handed the wheel over to God. I was going to let him be my pilot rather than my copilot. Not surprisingly, I met a nice Greek boy on the retreat; but most importantly, he was a devout Orthodox Christian. I felt like I had won the lottery.

After less than twenty-four hours of our meeting, he was convinced that we would be married within the next six months. For once, I wasn't turned off. I thought I'd give it a shot. The only problem I could foresee was that his name was also Carter. I enjoyed the attention and loved the fact that we had deep conversations about God. This is what was lacking in every single one of my other relationships.

It was no wonder that I was overjoyed and open to the relationship even though I wasn't completely attracted to him. As intense as the first twenty-four hours were, there was no way to describe the next few days.

Within the next five days, I felt like I got engaged, married, and divorced. The relationship zoomed to the finish line way too quickly. Don't get me wrong, Carter Maxos is a wonderful person. He was extremely generous and had a heart of gold, but he smothered and suffocated me with love. That's not healthy either.

I went from one extreme to the other. I truly see these relationships as learning opportunities.

> Day 1: He talked about marriage.
> Day 2: He talked about all the things I needed to work on and change in order to be a perfect girlfriend, although minutes before, he had said that the man who ended up with me would be the luckiest man alive because I'm such a catch.
> Day 3: He planned every weekend for the rest of the year with me with events.
> Day 4: He invited me to meet his family because he just knew he wanted to marry me.
> Day 5: I had had enough. I ended it, which sounds silly because it was such a short time. But like I said, he went from A to Z and skipped all the letters in between.

In the midst of his intricate directives, he still had time to constantly blow up my phone with his texts and phone calls. If he didn't get a response in a timely manner, which was a few minutes in his opinion, he would call or text again. By the time I actually got to my phone, I had a novel to hear or read. Additionally, his favorite catch phrase was, "I'm trying to be cute. Did it work?" I despise the word *cute* now because he killed it for me.

All hell broke loose when I told him I didn't think it would work. He said some pretty nasty things to me, which made me so relieved to be rid of him.

Here are some of the things he said to me:

"You are so messed up in the brain. You need counseling badly."

"You brought God into this. You're sacrilegious. You need to go to confession."

"You're a liar. How can you say that you want to make this work and then change your mind so quickly? You should have your teaching credentials revoked. I can't believe a liar such as yourself is teaching the future of our nation."

And my favorite (sarcasm, of course because this one stung, a lot): "I saw Carter Swinton's new girlfriend. She's blonde and has big boobs. She's hot. You guys are night and day. No wonder he left you for her. I don't even know what he was doing with you."

Ouch. That was digging into the depths of cruelty. I could definitely sense major hurt on his end, but how he dealt with it was unacceptable. I didn't deserve to hear any of what he said. Here's the kicker: He's thirty-five years old. That behavior isn't warranted at any age, but I could see it coming out of a teenager's mouth.

Realistically, I think *he* needed the counseling. And to think that he told me he was the best thing that would ever happen to me and that I would never find anyone better than him. I think deep down he knew that I was the best thing to happen to him, and he was trying to turn the tables around. The last thing he said to me on the phone was, "Thank God I didn't cut off all my ties with girls I was dating before you. By the way, I'm unfriending you on Facebook." *Please, make it official.*

Uhm, okay. I wasn't upset at all. What a bad taste he left in my mouth. Good riddance! But of course, I'm Lily, queen of stories, which means there was more. Immediately after the phone call, he texted me 27 times. I didn't respond to any of it. Crazy and psycho.

I seriously thought about changing my phone number and was so glad that he never found out where I lived. What a creeper. I felt sorry for him. All I could do for him was pray. The funny thing was that when I first told my dad about Carter Maxos, he was very wary, and his advice was, "Run for the hills! Drop him right now! What comes fast goes fast!" Boy, was he right.

That didn't work, so back to thoughts of Carter Swinton, I guess. Wait, no. I've made a change. I at least have to try *not* to think about him.

Life is funny. On paper, Carter Swinton was unbelievably perfect, raised in a well-to-do family, a holder of a postgraduate degree, popular and successful in school and life, liked by all. In reality, he was absolutely egocentric, morally inadequate, and a hater of faith.

Conversely, the best thing about Carter Maxos was that in reality, he was a dream (maybe not my dream, but good for someone else), loved God, completely devoted to his love interest. I later found out he had a rough childhood, never finished school, was unpopular all throughout life, and struggled in his family relationships. On paper, he was a mess.

Both Carters taught me a few lessons in their own right.

First impressions are not always correct and they can taint an entire world. A silly greeting card came to mind as I pondered that thought, "I will always cherish the initial misconceptions I had about you." Anyone can make themselves appear to be a certain way. Just because you're great on paper, doesn't necessarily mean your greatness transfers to reality and vice versa.

Initially, I unknowingly held on to Carter Swinton's first impression too tightly and even when I started seeing the light, I had already committed his first impression to my reality. I was responsible for making it exceptionally difficult to crawl my way back up to safety. I was drowning in my own fantasies. I was carrying my past in my pocket and letting it effect my future.

When I met Carter Maxos, I took the first impression with a grain of salt. I saved myself from a torrential outpour of ten years of unhealthy volatility. I saw the warning signs and paid attention to them.

Unfortunately, I held on to someone, Carter Swinton, who knew nothing of humility and empathy, and I gained absolutely no moral edification. There's no use trying to save anyone from themselves because all that will happen is that I will sink deeper and faster into the quicksand.

The hardest thing in life is to know which bridge to cross and which to burn. I need to burn both Carter bridges and never look back, just as in the Bible, Lot and his family were instructed by angels to run away from the evil of Sodom and Gomorrah and never turn back, lest they become a pillar of salt. Not to say that both Carters are evil, but that they are toxic fixtures in my life.

I was dangerously close to a fire that gave me no warmth but grew higher and hotter each passing year. Now that I finally feel the depths of my third-degree burns, I'm terrified of getting close to another fire, now that I've just begun to heal.

Chapter 23

I took a leap of faith and trusted that God would heal my wounds in due time. I was going to be an active participant in my healing as well. No wallowing.

Instead, I texted Grant Amar, a former high school classmate whom I reconnected with at my ten-year high school reunion about a month ago. He was thrilled to hear from me and asked me out to lunch that Sunday. Mind you, I met Carter Maxos on Saturday and broke up with him on Thursday. Three days later, Carter was forgotten, and I was on my way to bigger and better fish.

Grant was genuinely great. I've always known this about him. I knew him in high school through my friend Natalie. Grant and Natalie dated pretty seriously senior year of high school and into college with a tough breakup, which was why I would never have dreamed that our paths would cross.

I always had a little crush on him. What's funny is that I hadn't thought of him since the last time I saw him, which was with Natalie, more than ten years ago. It had been a while since

Grant and Natalie were together, so I guess it was okay that I was interested.

On a random note, the afternoon of my high school reunion, my sister asked me who I was most looking forward to running into at the reunion. For some reason, Grant Amar came to mind. And when I saw him, I was excited, and it seemed that he was equally excited to see me.

We got along so well and so easily. It was as if we were longtime friends just picking up where we left off. It turned out that he bought a house less than a mile away from where I bought my townhouse. We exchanged phone numbers and promised to hang out soon. I really enjoyed talking with him. I honestly never forgot about him even though he never contacted me. I had such a wonderful connection with him that I knew I'd be seeing him soon. So after the Carter Maxos ordeal, I decided to text him.

I really only expected lunch to be just that, a friendly lunch. Boy, was it more. He texted me the day before saying he couldn't wait for lunch, which led me to believe that he was interested in more than just friendship. He picked the time and place for lunch, which I loved. He took the initiative to take care of business.

Of course, he was there on time, sitting at the table. The instant I walked in and saw him, something happened. I felt like someone out of a movie. A movie where the woman walks into a restaurant and spots a man all alone, and her heart stops because she's struck by awe of his perfectness. That's exactly what happened.

I felt very connected and comfortable with him, and that's hard to find these days. We couldn't even find a break in our conversation to order, and we were starving. We were too busy talking with no awkward silences at all. After lunch was over, we were clearly not done hanging out, so we went for a walk. Then he invited me over to his house, where he gently grabbed my side and made me tingle. He had renovated his house by himself and kept asking me, "Do you love it?" I thought it was adorable that he kept asking. He's so sweet.

I've never dated anyone who's not a jerk. This was going to be a new experience for me. We then went to my townhouse, where he offered to help with any renovation work I was going to do.

Once again, he gently grabbed my side, and once again, I was tingling. I didn't want to leave him. The hug he gave me before we parted was so nice. It was long and inviting. I have no better words for it. It was just nice. I felt like I was finally home. My heart was smiling.

I found out that he was just as busy as I was and did so many of the same activities I did. We actually happened to be at the same places at the same time and never ran into each other.

We decided to meet up that Friday to watch a movie at his house. All week, Friday couldn't come fast enough. I really wanted to hang out with him. When he texted me Friday afternoon telling me he was sick, I was very disappointed. Nevertheless, I decided to go over anyway, and it was the best decision I made in a long time.

I think what I feel with Grant is true love. It's not sexual; it's just pure emotion. We were holding each other close and didn't want to let go of each other.

So here I am, never having expected to get over Carter Swinton. Just look at what he's done to me. Granted, I ultimately let those things happen.

I tried so desperately to love someone who just didn't reciprocate. It was like trying to catch the rain. Despite the hardships and pain I endured from Carter, my love for him will be forever. Look what you've done to me, Carter Swinton.

I can't make him love me. I can't make him care for me. What I do know is that I love him, whatever kind of love it is. I love him deeply. I am definitely a winner at this losing game, but the beauty of it, I know now, is that it's okay. I can still love someone with all I have but know that they are not right for me.

I always said I want to be with a Greek guy. I always said I want to be with an Orthodox man. I always said I want to be with someone who enjoys the same activities I enjoy. I always thought that guy would be Carter. He's Greek, but partakes in none of his Greek culture. He is Orthodox, but denounced the faith. He enjoys the same activities I enjoy but at a much more extreme and competitive capacity.

Ironically, Grant is half Greek and embraces his culture. Grant isn't religious but has always wanted to attend a Greek Orthodox church and learn more about the faith. Grant enjoys the same activities I enjoy, as we found out earlier when we attended many of the same functions without realizing it. God sure does have a sense of humor.

Five months after the Carter Swinton breakup, and I'm finally elated. I'm in a promising relationship with Grant Amar. He's responsible and so good to me. I could marry him. Above all, he makes me smile from the depths of my soul. I don't have to pretend around him. It all boils down to the right person thinking the sun shines out of your ass no matter what.

What I thought was impossible is now a reality with someone who was right under my nose all along. Looking back, I have to thank God. Looking forward, I put all my trust in God. All I can say is, "Thank you, God. You rock."

It always seems impossible, until it's done.

—Nelson Mandela

Epilogue

S itting next to the man I love in a cozy cabin, by a crackling fireplace, with the snow falling outside is the pleasant image that popped into my mind when Carter Swinton asked me to go snowboarding with him for the weekend. "My roommate rented a real big cabin in Mammoth on April 1-2. Thought I'd throw out the invite," Carter casually mentioned on instant messenger. I couldn't contain my excitement. "Yes!" I screamed to the computer. In my mind, we were already on the road.

Thank goodness he couldn't see the goofy grin plastered on my face or hear the overzealous enthusiasm in my voice. This would clearly be a missed opportunity if I didn't cancel all my weekend plans to join him. How could I refuse?

The whirlwind of thoughts that crowded my mind were completely irrational. *He's going to fall in love with me this weekend. He's going to introduce me to his friends as his girlfriend. He's going to spend all weekend snowboarding with me instead of his friends.*

The ping of a received message quickly snapped me out of my stupor. "Lily, you can't come, can you?" I hadn't timed it right. I didn't want to seem too eager, but now I had waited too long. I hurriedly typed, "How funny, that's the only weekend in April that I've got nothing going on. Ya, I'll go with you," I replied nonchalantly.

In reality, that was the only weekend in April completely booked with events. I unremorsefully cancelled dinner plans with my family, game night with my friends, and rescheduled my best friend's bridal shower just to share Carter with his friends for the weekend.

The irony of all this is that a year before, he left me to be with Brook. As far as I knew, she wasn't going to be joining us on the trip. This was going to be my second chance to get back with Carter.

There was no way I was going to jeopardize the weekend with bad conversation and out of trend clothes so I started writing a list of conversation topics and went on a very expensive shopping spree, buying new snowboarding gear and adorable clothes.

The night before the trip was disastrous. I couldn't eat, sleep or stop going to the bathroom. I was ridiculously excited. If my family didn't know about the trip, I'm sure they would have thought I was sick with the flu.

The plan was to get to his house by 5 a.m. to get an early start on the drive. That morning, when I woke up at 3 a.m., I had no problem jumping out of bed to get ready even though it was pitch black outside.

I took my time putting black eyeliner on, something I rarely do. I put on gray, skinny, distressed jeans to show off my trim figure and a lacey gray spaghetti strap tank top with a seductive, white, off-the-shoulder sweater. I topped the outfit off with my new, black, stylish winter boots and a beaded headband.

I was already imagining Carter looking me up and down the moment he set eyes on me in less than two hours. I was sure he would be nothing less than impressed with my fit physique and clothes that accentuated my assets. Mind you, I hadn't seen

Carter or spoken with him in over ten months. This was truly a big deal.

The forty-five minute drive to his house couldn't end fast enough. I parked my car in his garage and anxiously walked to his front door, already nervously sweating. The anticipation as he slowly opened the door was killing me. He stood there as gorgeous as ever, barefoot, in jeans and a white t-shirt.

Biting my lip, I looked him up and down, taking in his smoldering blue eyes and his haphazardly combed brown hair that gave him an air of sexiness, not hiding the fact that I was thrilled to see him.

He, on the other hand, didn't give me his usual seductive smirk, but rather hugged me emotionlessly. He didn't take his time to absorb the way I looked. He didn't say anything about not having seen me in ages. Something was off.

As I followed him into the house disheartened, I heard a girl's voice calling his name. I hoped that his roommate was a girl. But no such luck. It was Brook. She spent the night. He walked into his room and gave her a loud kiss. My heart dropped.

The little food that I had the night before was finding its way to my mouth. I felt sick. I was sure that I had been invited to Mammoth in an attempt for Carter to get back with me.

As I uncomfortably waited in his living room, I tried to even my heavy breathing. I couldn't let him know that I was still in love with him. I was going to have to be the friend all weekend.

Brook never came out of the bedroom and I never saw her, but I could hear her. We were mortal enemies without ever meeting. She disliked me because I dated Carter before her and I disliked, more like despised, her because she stole the love of my life from me.

I was thoroughly confused. Why was she there? Nothing made sense to me anymore. If she spent the night, why wasn't she going on the trip and why was I going instead? Suddenly, I didn't want to go with Carter anymore.

One point for Brook, zero for me. Little did I know that this was only hurdle number one of many to come.

Carter and I finally left that hell-hole and got on the road. I tried to cheer myself up knowing that we were going to spend the five hour drive to the mountains, just the two of us, *alone*. I was a little hesitant to give myself a point but a point by default is still a point, not that I'm counting. I'm back in the game. Watch out Brook! Lily has arrived!

During my shopping spree I also decided to buy snacks for the road. You know, the best way to get to a man's heart is through his stomach. I was determined to win him back.

Despite the churning in my stomach and my hunger pangs from the lack of food the previous day, we had some pretty good conversation over some delicious snacks. We talked about his job at a new law firm, my first home purchase, my plans of going back to school to become a kinesiologist, my surfing trip to Bali, and his obsession with Formula One racing, just to name a few.

Things were looking up. We were laughing and getting to know each other all over again. I was reminded of how much I enjoy being around him. He just makes me smile like no one else can. The way he looks at me out of the corner of his eye, trying to stifle his laughter when I'm being cute and silly. The way his fingers linger on my arm when he's making a point.

My boots and socks were littered all over the floor of the passenger side; I was finally at ease. To my dismay, we had to pause our conversation to get gas. As we pulled into a gas station and he got out of the car to pump gas, I could feel the magical rekindling of our relationship disappear. In an attempt to keep any conversation going, I offered to give him my debit card to pay for gas.

Just as I was about to give Carter my pin number, because I was too comfortable to get out of the car, a brief moment of sanity kicked in. Had I revealed my pin number, his birthday, Carter would have driven me right back home, I'm sure. My mind turns to mush when I'm around him. As I started to put my shoes on to punch in my pin number, Carter, without any hesitation, wrapped his arms around my waist, picked me up out of the car, and drew me near to him.

Our faces were inches apart, breathing the same air; I could feel the temperature rising rapidly. Unwillingly, I turned away from him to type in my four digit code. As I turned back, I let out a gasp, his burning gaze leaving me breathless. He carried me back to the car once the tank was full and ended our short-lived rendezvous.

He definitely wanted to get his hands on me and now I was sure of it. Now that we were away from home and away from Brook, anything was possible.

Let the games begin. He is ready to have me back in his life. That's another point for Lily on the scoreboard. Who's got Carter now, Brook?

We got back on the road, with the magic revived. The attraction was definitely there. Shortly after my victory, Carter got a text from Brook saying she was in love with another man.

I'm sure the look on my face was a dead giveaway that I was ecstatic. This was too easy. I wasn't even going to have to try to get my man back. Carter proceeded to show me the text Brook sent.

To my surprise, it was only a picture of the word Noah, Noah's Bagels. I just about died. Carter totally manipulated that situation.

Maybe there were three of us in this game. Carter was on the scoreboard now too, but with a dagger attached to his point. It was a cheap point and he knew it.

I blew it off, or so I thought, until he started talking about Brook. "She's going shopping for a wedding dress today." Although I knew he was pulling my leg, more like ripping it out, in that split second, my face was a dead giveaway that I was truly upset.

He paused just long enough to catch my disappointment and followed up with, "It's for her best friend." He was on a roll.

"Brook and I are planning a trip to Mexico. You should come with us. Maybe then she'll like you," Carter facetiously said. This was torture. *What are you doing Carter?! That's two points for you. You don't even have a reason to play this game. You're the one we're fighting over.* He knows how to get under my skin; I'll give him that.

Why the tides changed, I'll never know. We were only an hour into the five hour drive and I already felt defeated. My initial plans of winning him back were long gone. How could I win when he's the master of this game that he's created?

Hurdle number two was tortuous, long and drawn out. There were jagged edges all along the hurdle as it stood menacingly in a wide puddle of murky water.

I had a goal to win him back this weekend; I couldn't and I wouldn't let Carter get to me. I had come to an impasse, but I'm no loser. I dug deep and found the strength to brush off every crude, hurtful, and deceitful comment Carter directed at me the rest of the drive. Four hours later, we made it to the snow, minus my dignity.

The scoreboard was littered with undeserving points to Brook, Carter, and me. Points by default, stolen points, cheap points.

Somehow, the moment we got out of the car and into the snow, there was an unspoken agreement to cease fire. I couldn't have been more thankful. I was extremely exhausted and the weekend had barely begun.

We enjoyed a nice breakfast together and went snowboarding. He's much better than I am, but he stayed all day with me, teaching me tricks and helping me improve my technique. I thought that was sweet. Was I reading into it too much? Probably, but I didn't care.

I was finally enjoying myself. I could have watched him snowboard all day. As he came down the mountain, I was mesmerized by his body turning from side to side effortlessly, while he smiled at me deviously.

After a long day of snowboarding, we went into the cabin, took a short nap together, read out loud to each other, and played cards. We were finally enjoying each other's company with no pretenses. His friends still hadn't arrived and I was just fine with that.

We went out to lunch then decided to sit in the spa to relax where he had an inclination to give me a massage. Although I despised Brook, I'm no home-wrecker, but in that moment I didn't care if the massage wasn't harmless. Carter grabbed my sides and slowly pulled me back into him, further intensifying the anticipation.

As his fingers found their way down my back and underneath the strings of my bikini, the heavier his breathing down my neck became. I wanted Carter back and I quickly discovered my devious nature; I would stop at nothing.

As the day continued, Brook was less and less on his mind. His flirting became less witty and more obvious. There was no way of mistaking his intentions.

We decided to cook dinner together rather than go out to eat. Romantic, right? We were in the small kitchen listening to country music, preparing food, bumping into each other, feeding each other, and randomly hugging.

It was a perfect end to a perfect day, minus the drive. I was sure we were back on. We were thoroughly enjoying each other's company. The chemistry was there. You can't make that stuff up. It was real! I gave up keeping count on the scoreboard because I was sure I was in the lead. When you're that far ahead, everyone else's score doesn't matter.

I was enveloped in his arms, seductively feeding him an apple when the cabin door opened and the atmosphere changed. Just like that, the romance was blown out the door. I could hear the gust of magic as it rustled past my ear, its tendrils artfully maneuvering around Carter's friends, taunting me, and quickly leaving without so much as a whisper.

Carter took a step away from me just before his friends could witness the heat between us. Instantaneously, we went back to being friends. In my disappointment, I turned in early that night. I wanted to go to bed and dream vividly about my amazing day with Carter.

I didn't dream about Carter. I didn't sleep. Instead, I planned. I knew that he was waking up earlier than his friends on Saturday to get an early start on snowboarding. I set my alarm for 6 a.m. Of course, sleep never came to me. I laboriously watched the clock, anxiously awaiting 6 a.m. At 6 a.m. on the dot, I applied some eyeliner and smudged it a bit to look like remnants from last night. At 6:01, I casually opened my bedroom door and went to the kitchen to get a glass of water.

Just as I thought, I was the first one up. At 6:04, Carter walked into the kitchen and saw me staring out the bay window with my back turned to him. I had strategically positioned myself to be able to see his reflection in the window without him seeing my face. I knew by his goofy grin that he was happy to see me.

I slowly turned around, sure that Carter would embrace me. He did nothing of the sort. When we finally made eye contact, all traces of his grin were gone. "Morning Lily. What are you doing up so early?" Not an inkling of yearning for me could be found. Dumbfounded, words could not escape my mouth. "Well, I gotta get ready. I want to be one of the first ones on the mountain. Have a good day," he said as he hurriedly walked away.

That's all I got! That's it! I didn't imagine it! I know that grin. It's Carter's grin of desire.

Most of Saturday was a blur. Carter spent most of the day snowboarding with his friends, occasionally checking in with me through text. I boarded solo since he and his friends were experts and I was still a beginner. We all met up for lunch, but he was too engrossed storytelling about his stunts that morning that I was practically invisible. I don't think I said one word at the meal.

After lunch, I went back to snowboarding solo and headed home a few hours later. I was exhausted. I lost sleep attempting to reel him back in; my efforts gone to waste. Of course, I was the first one back so I took my time showering and styling my hair. At least I would look nice when Carter came back. Without Carter, I was unhappy.

Once again, Carter didn't seem impressed to see me. I had forgotten how self-righteous and absorbed he could get in the presence of his friends. Dinner was eventless. I contributed a few witty comments, but I was still mostly invisible.

That night, all his friends went out to bars while Carter and I stayed in the cabin in front of the fireplace. We were sitting on the couch, our legs plastered against each other, his left hand resting on my thigh. I was sure he wanted to stay in with me for a salacious evening. Saturday looked like it could perk up and redeem itself. My initial daydream was coming true.

Wouldn't you know, he easily rammed the mood to the complete other end of the spectrum when he started venting to me about Brook, as if we were best friends. He pulled away from me, creating a painful void between us. "Why is Brook always upset with me? I try to be the boyfriend she wants me to be, but I just can't make her happy. I've tried everything. Lily, help me. You know me better than anyone else does. What should I do?"

Throughout his complaining, he would throw in comments like, "I wish she were more like you. You're such a good person." The back-handed compliments stunned me.

While I was honored that he trusted me with this information, considering our past, and appreciated me as a whole, I was seething inside. He seriously wanted my honest advice. What could I do but help the man I love get through tough times with his girlfriend?

I read that situation very wrong. He stayed in because he was depressed about Brook. I still didn't understand why he invited me on the trip. The setting was perfect, the chemistry was there, yet he refused to see what was right underneath his nose. Let the irony begin.

Shortly afterwards, his friends returned from the bar. Despite their drunken stupor, they could sense the heaviness in the air between Carter and me. One of the guys mentioned the deep connection he noted between us and pointed out that Carter seemed happy with me. But he wasn't sure what to make of it since Carter was dating Brook, who constantly upset him.

I was irate. When outsiders are perceptive enough to see the situation for what it really is and the player, ahem Carter, cannot, that irritates me.

Another one of the guys brought home a married woman. To my surprise, Carter reprimanded his friend and lectured him about fidelity. I almost laughed out loud, but I was too angry from his friend's earlier comment about our connection. *But Carter, you've been unfaithful to Brook since yesterday.*

After that situation got sorted out, we all went to bed in our respective bedrooms. Just as I was falling asleep, Carter texted me saying he wished he could be next to me. *So be next to me! It's not like you haven't crossed every other line with me.* For the next hour, we texted back and forth; me trying to convince him to stay with me and him battling his desire to join me. In the end, we both went to bed unhappy in an attempt to try to do the right thing for the first time that weekend. Needless to say, we both had restless sleep. To this day, his logic is a mystery to me.

Then Sunday came: the drive home. It was a sad day. Only five more hours to spend together until who knows when. This entire weekend was completely out of the blue. It could be another ten months before seeing him again. Not only was my mission to win Carter back unaccomplished, but I also felt like our relationship regressed. We were back to where we were before we started dating: nowhere.

I gratefully said goodbye to his friends as we loaded the car; I was anxious to be completely alone with Carter again. As the hours we had left together were dwindling, he suggested we stop at some natural hot springs on the way home. I was so appreciative for the extra hour to spend with Carter.

We were sitting across from each other in the steamy springs, talking about the weekend sadly ending. Carter was fidgeting around and suddenly, the next thing I knew, his board shorts were laying out on a rock next to us. He got naked! "That way when I get out, my board shorts will already be dry, and I won't be in wet clothes," he said in response to the look of disbelief on my face. He looked at me like I was crazy for not following that logic. *You're testing every single one of my limits.*

Here I was, in the dreamy secluded wilderness, sitting in a hot spring next to the completely naked man I love, and I couldn't do anything about it. This had to be hell. There went any coherent conversation.

My mind was racing with possibilities in this scenario, none of which were viable because the shadow of Brook was looming over me. My only saving grace was the brown rocks that darkened the pristine water, enough for me not to see his nakedness.

Because it wasn't already hot enough in this hell he created for me, Carter got out of the hot spring and started walking around for a reason unbeknownst to me. I couldn't fathom his absurdity. Not only was I infuriated, but I was also worried that at any point someone could come and see him pantless in a public place.

All I could see were the rapid flicker of lights on the scoreboard as Carter's score shot up infinitely. As I tried my best to keep my eyes from roaming, he tried his best to get my eyes to roam.

No matter what I wanted to happen, I knew he would never take responsibility for any of his actions. I would be the one at fault. I quickly reminded myself of his comment the previous night, "You're such a good person," and immediately made a decision not to let my attraction get in the way of doing the right thing.

It seemed as though Carter's admiration and respect for my goodness was a double edged sword. While he appreciated it, he also wanted to devour it. He wanted to single-handedly be the catalyst to my fall, all in the name of his ego. I wasn't going to let him take me down. Eventually, he gave up the game, put his board shorts back on, and we walked back to the car in silence.

I needed retaliation. I tactlessly got in the car in just my miniscule bikini for the rest of the drive home. He was distracted, just as I'd hoped. As long as I kept my hands off of him, I wasn't at fault. I didn't have a boyfriend to report to so I was shameless.

We sat in silence for what seemed an eternity. I wouldn't break. I needed to win this battle, at least just once. Immodestly, I started rubbing lotion onto my arms, legs, and chest making sure to slowly massage my body in circular motions. Gotcha! I caught him taking a sideways glance, trying his hardest not to look. This was no match he was going to win.

Without taking his eyes off the road, he placed his hand on my thigh and continued rubbing the lotion in. After a few moments, he let out a long exasperated breath, after holding it in for so long. He couldn't keep his hands off me. "I miss this. I miss touching you," he softly said. I pulled away. "You had this, Carter. Why did you leave?" No answer.

He placed his hand back on my thigh. I pulled away again. "Just let me touch you for a little bit. I haven't touched any girl other than Brook for the last ten months. This doesn't count. I know you," he said desperately. "This is cheating and you know it, Carter," I said agitated. His irrationality was getting on my nerves. We sat in silence as my blood boiled and steam emanated from my pores.

Somewhere in the blur of the drive home, Brook texted Carter and he texted back while driving at unsafe speeds. I was enraged that he would put my life in danger over a text. I reprimanded him and told him I didn't want him texting while driving.

When Brook called later wondering why he stopped responding to her texts, he immediately told her that I didn't want him texting her. There was a plethora of safe excuses he could have used such as, "it's against the law," "it's unsafe," or "I'd rather hear your voice." He was setting us up against each other for no good reason except that he could.

Once again, just a few hours into the drive and I was already exhausted. "Put some clothes on; we're almost home. My roommate might be home; he might think stuff happened with us," Carter blandly said, breaking the silence, a few miles before we reached his place. *But stuff did happen with us!*

My irritated response was, "You live on the beach. I'm allowed to wear a bikini at the beach." He dropped the subject.

In my final attempt to rack some points, while he was unloading the car, I yanked out some of my distinctive, dark, curly hair and put it underneath the passenger seat, wrapped it around the passenger seatbelt, tucked it into the cushions of the backseat, and for good measure, placed some on the driver's seat. Brook was sure to find my hair and be reminded of me.

As the perfect weekend gone bad was coming to a close, Carter helped carry my luggage to my car and gave me an intimate hug. "Will I see you next week at the Easter picnic?" he casually asked as if there was no animosity between us. I was caught off guard, and coyly nodded.

With a half-smile tugging at my lips, I got in my car and excitedly wondered what next week would bring.